SOUTHERN LIFE IN FICTION

SOUTHERN LIFE IN FICTION

JAY B. HUBBELL

EUGENIA DOROTHY BLOUNT LAMAR MEMORIAL LECTURES, 1959

Delivered at Mercer University on November 17, 18, and 19

UNIVERSITY OF GEORGIA PRESS
ATHENS

Library of Congress Catalog Card Number: 60-9898

Printed in the United States of America

FOOTE & DAVIES, INC., ATLANTA

FOR

DAVID

AND

BARBARA

Contents

Foreword

WITH THE PUBLICATION OF THIS THIRD SERIES OF EUGENIA Dorothy Blount Lamar Memorial Lectures, delivered at Mercer University in November, 1959, the Lamar Lecture Committee and the University reaffirm their gratitude to the late Mrs. Lamar's wisdom and generosity in endowing this perpetual series of lectures. Mrs. Lamar, a cultural leader in Macon and the South for nearly three-quarters of a century, was keenly interested in the continuation of traditional Southern values amid the kaleidoscope of social and economic changes taking place in the modern South. She left a legacy to Mercer University with the request that it be used "to provide lectures of the very highest type of scholarship which will aid in the permanent preservation of the values of Southern culture, history, and literature."

Though the metaphor is well worn, it is difficult to avoid a comparison between the third Lamar Lecturer, Jay Broadus Hubbell, and Tennyson's Ulysses. Professor Hubbell, author of the monumental *The South in American Literature, The Last Years of Henry Timrod,* and other books and articles, is vigorous and productive in retirement. This scholar, a pioneer in the study of American literature and the first editor of the quarterly *Ameri-*

can Literature, does not "rust unburnished," but continues to "shine in use," as Tennyson put it. Professor Hubbell is also a link between the old and the new. A few days before he delivered the Lamar Lectures he told an audience at a language association meeting of having heard Thomas Wentworth Higginson read poems imitative of the way Higginson had heard Poe read them. This incident, which had happened over fifty years ago in Boston, gave Professor Hubbell a living link with Poe that no other scholar shared in the symposium on the Virginia poet. Yet, when Professor Hubbell arrived at Mercer University, he was driving a Falcon, one of the newest wrinkles in the auto-maker's art. Somehow it was fittingly symbolic of a latter-day Ulysses.

BENJAMIN W. GRIFFITH, JR., *Chairman*
The Lamar Lecture Committee

Mercer University
Macon, Georgia

Preface

THESE LECTURES, WHICH WERE DELIVERED AT MERCER UNIversity on November 17, 18, and 19, 1959, under the title "Southern Life in Fact and Fiction," were addressed to somewhat different audiences: the first, to the English staff, students, and their guests; the second, to the University faculty; and the third, to the Lamar Lecture Committee and the general public. A fourth lecture, "The Civil War in Literature," not included in this volume, was given in the student assembly.

The general theme of these lectures is one that has long interested me: the function of literature as a reflection of the life of the American people, a subject which of course involves some study of the various interrelations of literature and history. The reasons for my emphasis upon Virginia and Georgia in the second and third lectures will be obvious to anyone who reads them. The first lecture, except for the omission of one passage, is printed substantially as it was delivered; the second and third lectures have undergone some revision.

I wish to express my sense of the honor in being chosen as the Lamar Lecturer of 1959 following Donald

Davidson and Bernard Mayo, two scholars whose work I greatly admire. I am indebted to Professor Benjamin W. Griffith, Chairman of the Lamar Lecture Committee, and his colleagues for the many courtesies shown to Mrs. Hubbell and me during our stay in Macon.

JAY B. HUBBELL

Durham, North Carolina
January 4, 1960

LECTURE

ONE

An Imperfect Mirror, Or Fiction and Fact

IN MOLIERE'S DELIGHTFUL COMEDY, *Le Bourgeois Gentilhomme,* M. Jourdain learns from his tutor that since he is unwilling to write to his sweetheart in verse, he must write his letter in prose. And so the bourgeois gentleman discovers to his amazement that all his life he has been speaking nothing but prose. M. Jourdain may stand for us as a symbol of mankind. In the beginning and for ages thereafter all literature was poetry. Literary prose was a late discovery; until the eighteenth century artistic prose fiction as we know it hardly existed; and the artistic short story looks very much like a creation of the nineteenth century. Verse was for ages the prescribed medium not only for the lyric poem but also for drama and narrative, whether history or fiction. In the past two and a half centuries, however, prose has more and more crowded out verse as the story-teller's medium. In our time the poets have all but lost their audience. The novelists, on the other hand, have found many more readers and a far more remunerative market for their wares.

And yet for a whole generation we have been told that the novel is an obsolescent literary genre. It is, we are informed, being rapidly displaced by the radio, the motion picture, and now by television—any one of which can supply the craving for fiction much more painlessly than a novel by Ellen Glasgow or William Faulkner. And as for the current best-sellers, why should we bother to read them when, if we wait a little while, we shall be able to see them on the screen or, if we must read them, condensed versions will shortly be made available. A century and more ago Emerson and his friend Carlyle were hopefully predicting that novels would be superseded by biographies and autobiographies. Carlyle wrote in his essay on Diderot:

> . . . were it not reasonable to prophesy that this exceeding great multitude of Novel-writers and such like, must, in a new generation, gradually do one of two things: either retire into nurseries, and work for children, minors and semi-fatuous persons of both sexes; or else, what were far better, sweep their Novel-fabric into the dust-cart, and betake themselves with such faculty as they have to understand and record what is *true,*—of which surely there is, and will forever be, a whole Infinitude unknown to us, of infinite importance to us!

There are so many bad novels on the market that sometimes one wishes that Carlyle's prophecy had been fulfilled. In paperback editions American readers are buying novels by the million; and the magazines, slick and pulp alike, are still running serials and short stories. From the point of view of author, publisher, reader, and critic, prose fiction appears to have more vitality than any other literary type. In the twentieth century, writers who if they had lived in an earlier age would have been poets, playwrights, or essayists have turned to prose fiction because it is at once the most influential and the most profitable type of writing. It is hardly surprising that so many poets have tried their hands at novel-writing with varying degrees of success. Sidney Lanier, who once had great hopes of his only novel, came to regard *Tiger-Lilies* as a failure; but DuBose Heyward succeeded so well with *Porgy* that he practically abandoned poetry. The novel has attracted writers whose greatest talents are not in the way of narrative. Some of them seem not to know that the primary function of the novelist is to tell a story. The novel has attracted journalists, reformers, and amateurs of various kinds who care nothing for the novel as an art form. What they want is an audience and a substantial income.

Not more than one novel in ten thousand has any claim to our attention as students of American literature. Yet one must never make the mistake of ignoring subliterary fiction, for it is a power in the world. Indeed, so powerful an influence is prose fiction that one might alter old Andrew Fletcher's well-known comment on the ballad to read: "Let me write a nation's novels and I care not who makes its laws." Do you remember how at a White House reception President Lincoln greeted the author of *Uncle Tom's Cabin*? He said: "So this is the little lady who made this big war!" Where do we get our notions of life on the antebellum Southern plantation if not from fiction? It is the writers of fiction that have given us Uncle Tom and Uncle Remus, Ole Marster and Ole Miss, Colonel Grangerford and Simon Legree. Ask the next man you meet for his conception of the New England Puritans and you will probably get a blurred image which derives ultimately from Nathaniel Hawthorne's vivid but inaccurate portraits of the men and women who lived in Colonial Boston and Salem. It was James Fenimore Cooper who fixed for us—and even more for the Europeans—the popular conception of the American Indian. Bret Harte gave us the image of the California miner, and there it is today in the Westerns of the movies, television, and the pulp magazines.

The English novel grew up with little benefit from formal literary criticism. The critics were concerned mainly with what seemed to them the chronically low estate of poetry, and they failed to see that the novel—diffuse and formless though it often was—had become the most important of literary genres. In the 1880's, however, there began a vigorous debate, still continuing, about the aims and the methods of the novel and the short story. In an article in the *Century Magazine* in November, 1882, William Dean Howells irritated the English when he said: "The art of fiction has, in fact, become a finer art than it was with Dickens and Thackeray." What Howells meant was that Henry James was a finer artist than any of the older English novelists. In the eighties and nineties leading writers, like Howells, James, Stevenson, Maupassant, and Zola, put into print their best thinking about the art of fiction. In our own time illuminating criticism has come from Ellen Glasgow, Edith Wharton, Virginia Woolf, E. M. Forster, and many others. And yet for all this dissection of the art of the novelist, one notes the same wide disagreement over fundamental questions as one finds among critics of poetry and drama from the time of Plato and Aristotle down to that of T. S. Eliot and John Crowe Ransom.

Not long ago I read with fascination the published correspondence of H. G. Wells and Henry James. Wells was an Englishman of the lower middle class and a reformer who finally decided that he was not an artist but a journalist. James was an artist, an American, and—it is important to remember—a gentleman. Of James, Wells wrote in his autobiography: "One could not be in a room with him for ten minutes without realizing the importance he attached to the dignity of this art of his. . . . But I," Wells continued, "was disposed to regard a novel as about as much an art form as a market place or a boulevard. It had not even necessarily to get anywhere. You went by it on your various occasions." As the older and more experienced writer, the wise and kindly James gave Wells the benefit of the criticism of an expert craftsman. This great service Wells finally repaid by publishing *Boon,* an ill-natured satire attacking the ideal of fiction which he thought James represented. When James discovered that his friend and protégé had publicly branded him as "extraordinarily futile" and had resolved him into "an unmitigable mistake," he gave up all hope of Wells. In a memorable final letter he protested: "But I *have* no view of life and literature, I maintain, other than that our form of the latter in especial is admirable exactly by its range and variety, its plasticity and liberality, its fairly living on the sincere and shifting experiences of the individual practitioner." Joseph Conrad, who like James had tried to help Wells, also broke with him. "The difference between us, Wells, is fundamental," he wrote. "You don't care for humanity but think they are to be improved. I love humanity but know they are not."

Henry James might be described as the novelists' novelist, for he taught secrets of craftsmanship to many writers—among them, Wells, Conrad, Howells, Hamlin

Garland, Owen Wister, Edith Wharton, and Willa Cather—each of whom found more readers than James ever had. Beyond question James was a great artist, and yet there are artistic shortcomings even in the novels of the master's final phase. In *A Backward Glance* Edith Wharton, who knew him better perhaps than any other writer knew him, tells us that wishing better to understand his system, she unwittingly asked him some very embarrassing questions: "What was your idea in suspending the four principal characters in 'The Golden Bowl' in the void? What sort of life did they lead when they were not watching each other, and fencing with each other? Why have you stripped them of all the *human fringes* we necessarily trail after us through life?" The master looked at Mrs. Wharton in pained surprise and said in a disturbed voice: "My dear—I didn't know I had!"

In the third act of *Hamlet* there is a famous passage which many an English teacher has quoted in order to emphasize the obligation of the serious novelist to tell the truth about life. Hamlet is talking about the actor's art: " . . . whose end, both at the first and now, was and is, to hold, as 'twere, the mirror up to nature; to show virtue her own feature, scorn her own image, and the very age and body of the time his [its] form and pressure."

Now the art of acting and the art of the novelist involve the use of two quite different mediums; and the novelist, no matter how eager he may be to tell the whole truth about life, employs a mirror which in inexpert hands is likely to give back a very imperfect reflection. The essence of art is selection. Our daily lives are full of details which are, for the particular purpose of the novelist, meaningless or dull. If his picture is to have meaning, he must select and rearrange and employ lights and shadows so that his readers cannot fail to see the significant things he himself has seen.

There are many factors which may becloud the mirror and prevent the novelist from giving us anything like a comprehensive picture of life. The writer, young or old, is limited by his temperament, his taste, and his talent, by literary tradition, by fashion and convention, by the policies of his editors and his publishers, perhaps also by those of the book clubs and the Hollywood moguls, and by what he knows or imagines of the desires of those who may read his stories. The world is full of magnificent literary materials, but most of them are not for him; he simply cannot use effectively more than a tiny fraction of them. His personal experience, which is a large part of his working capital, is severely limited; and generally he can make no use of the hints for stories offered by sympathetic friends. Some aspects of the life he knows best he cannot use because his publisher has told him they are not acceptable to potential purchasers of his books. The successful novelist may be able to induce his publisher to accept unconventional materials, but the beginner had better stick to well-tried formulas and conventional ingredients. If, however, he elects to follow his own instincts and seek the approval of the intelligent few whose opinion he values most, he will probably have to pay the printer's bill himself or forego publication. That may be the nobler course; but even if his book is published, he will be lucky if it is noticed in any reputable newspaper or magazine. What editor, publisher, book clubs, and general reader all seem to want is usually only pleasant fictions about human nature and society. Fortunately there is a small minority of intelligent readers who demand of the novelist fine workmanship and a good story which reveals something new and significant drawn from the infinite variety of human nature and human experience.

In the latter half of the nineteenth century journalists and other literary prophets were calling vociferously for the Great American Novel, which might more appropriately have been called the Great American Delusion. In one great novel was to be held up to the admiration of the world the American way of life in North and South, East and West. It was at the same time to be a tale which could hold boys and girls from the play-ground and old men from the chimney corner. No one among the advocates of the Great American Novel seems to have thought of asking the relevant questions: Where is the Great French Novel? What is the Great English or Russian or German Novel? There is of course no such thing. An admirer of Tolstoy might perhaps argue that *War and Peace* is the Great Russian Novel; but if so, what are we to do with his *Anna Karénina,* probably an even greater novel than *War and Peace*? Even in the many volumes of his *Comédie humaine* the great Balzac was not able to do for France all that naive American journalists were demanding of a single novelist. Human life is so rich, so complex, and sometimes so intractable that no American novelist has ever been able to give us a complete picture of one small town, much less of a great city like New York.

In "What Paul Bourget Thinks of Us" Mark Twain wrote: "There is only one expert who is qualified to examine the souls and the life of a people and make a valuable report—the native novelist." A foreign observer, like Paul Bourget, he said, could picture American life as seen from the outside; but no foreigner could "report its interior—its soul, its life, its speech, its thought." A knowledge of these things, said Mark Twain,

> is acquirable in only one way—not two or four or six—*absorption;* years and years of unconscious absorption; years and years of intercourse with the life concerned; of living it, indeed; sharing personally in its shames and prides, its joys and griefs, its loves and hates, its prosperities and reverses, its shows and shabbinesses, its deep patriotisms, its whirlwinds of political passion, its adorations—of flag, and heroic dead, and the glory of the national name.

Only thus could the native novelist prepare himself to give us in Allen Tate's fine phrase "knowledge carried to the heart."

Mark Twain was perhaps thinking of the Great American Novel when he said:

> Does the native novelist try to generalize the nation? No, he lays plainly before you the ways and speech and life of a few people grouped in a certain place—his own place—and that is one book. In time he and his brethren will report to you the life and the people of the whole nation—the life of a group in a New England village; in a New York village; in a Texan village; in an Oregon village; in villages in fifty states and territories; then the farm-life in fifty states and territories; a hundred patches of life and groups of people in a dozen widely separated cities. . . . And when a thousand able novels have been written, *there* you have the soul of the people, the life of the people, the speech of the people; and not anywhere else can these be had. And the shadings of character, manners, feelings, ambitions, will be infinite.

There is truth in what Mark Twain has so well said, but I think we need to be reminded that novelists, like poets and show people of all kinds, are given to exaggerating the importance of their respective arts. There are economists, sociologists, and historians who would dispute Mark Twain's claim that the native novelist is the "one expert who is qualified to examine the souls and the life of a people and make a valuable report." There are also pollsters who would gladly take on the job if the fee offered were large enough.

Mark Twain, who was irritated by Paul Bourget's criticisms of American life, underestimated the ability of the outsider to understand and record the life of a region or a nation. Until after the Civil War few Southern writers had any genuine appreciation of the fine and varied literary materials all about them. Thackeray and Mrs. Stowe are only the best known of numerous Northern and European authors of novels and travel books who helped to make Americans aware of their rich heritage in the Southern states. In the years that followed the Civil War, Constance Fenimore Woolson, John W. De Forest, and Albion W. Tourgée, each of whom had spent several years in the South, wrote novels and short stories which portray for us aspects of Southern life not vividly painted by our Southern novelists.

The composite picture of life in the South painted by Mark Twain and his contemporaries is a very vivid one. It contains some memorable portraits of Southern men and women, black and white, and some fine pictures of Southern backgrounds. But there are large and important aspects of Southern life which have little or no part in the total picture. The Southern writers of fiction had much to tell us of life in Virginia, Georgia, Louisiana, Kentucky, and Tennessee; but they had little to say about the Carolinas, Alabama, Mississippi, Florida, Arkansas, and Texas.

The composite portrait of the South painted by Joel Chandler Harris, Thomas Nelson Page, and their fellows has other limitations. They were interested primarily in the Old South. Even when they were writing about the New South, their characters are chiefly types that belonged to the old regime: old soldiers and their families struggling with poverty in an alien political and economic order. Their ex-slaves are house servants, not the far more numerous field hands. The novelists almost ignored the yeomen farmers, who were the great bulk of the white population. The mood of the writers was nostalgic and romantic. They gave us a highly idealized picture of Southern life. If a novelist treated realistically the relations between the races, he was likely, as George W. Cable discovered, to find himself denounced as a Southern Yankee.

One who wants a comprehensive picture of Southern life must not limit his reading to the novelists of any one period. In the twentieth century our Southern writers have emphasized just those aspects of life which the writers of the New South neglected. Romance has yielded place to realism and realism to naturalism. In the novels of Ellen Glasgow, Thomas Wolfe, and William Faulkner one finds in the foreground character types which in the stories of James Lane Allen and Thomas Nelson Page appeared only in the dim background. And yet the twentieth-century novelists also have their blind spots, their aversions, and their illusions, though it is naturally more difficult for us to recognize them. Fashion is a very potent influence in fiction as in dress and manners, and it is difficult to distinguish what is permanent from what is temporary and perishable.

The South has long been more conscious of its past than either the North or the West, and thus it is not surprising that the historical novel has been a favorite form with Southern writers. Many of our local-color novels and short stories have historical settings. The historical novel, however, has no high standing with either historians or literary critics. For Brander Matthews and many other critics it has been a bastard form and neither good literature nor authentic history. Nevertheless, as Ernest Bernbaum pointed out in *PMLA* some years ago, few of the critics who condemn the historical novel in the abstract will deny merit to *The Heart of Midlothian, Henry Esmond, Romola, War and Peace, The Scarlet Letter, The Prince and the Pauper, The Grandissimes,* and *So Red the Rose.* Nor will the critics deny merit to the many great historical dramas beginning with Shakespeare and ending with T. S. Eliot.

The traditional departmentalization of the fields of knowledge in our college curriculums tends to obscure their manifold interrelations, and this is especially true in the fields of history and literature. In what I shall say on this subject I speak only as a literary historian with a special interest in the life and thought of the people of the Southern states. In my published work I am deeply indebted to the historians of the twentieth century, most of them Southerners, who have given us a new and much more accurate and comprehensive account of life in the South from the time of Captain John Smith to that of Franklin D. Roosevelt. Let me mention two of them: the late Ulrich B. Phillips, who, though for many years lived and taught in the North, was a native of Georgia; and E. Merton Coulter, a native of North Carolina, who has made for himself a distinguished career at the University of Georgia.

In these days there are historians that remind me of Francis Bacon, who in his youth took all knowledge for his province. This broadened interpretation of the field of the historian seems to me on the whole a good thing.

And yet there is a danger. The historian who, like Oswald Spengler or Arnold Toynbee, ventures into the wide field of literary culture or the history of the fine arts may discover to his chagrin that his friends who have specialized in those subjects regard his taste and judgment as untrustworthy. I have found myself disposed to question the literary taste of certain distinguished American historians whom I shall not name.

Some of you may have read in *The South in American Literature* my brief chapter on "Sir Walter Scott and the South." If so, you may have been amazed as I was to discover how many eminent historians—Charles A. Beard and William E. Dodd among them—have endorsed Mark Twain's "wild proposition" that the Waverley romances exerted so profound an influence upon antebellum Southern life that Scott may be held responsible for the Civil War. So far as I know not one of these historians offered or even asked for any evidence to back up this theory propounded by a novelist who did not like Scott. If Sir Walter was responsible for the Civil War, I somewhat facetiously suggested, that malign influence could have come only through *Uncle Tom's Cabin*. Before she wrote that novel, Mrs. Stowe had read *Ivanhoe* no less than nine times.

Novels and plays can yield to the historian important information about the ideals and the way of life of a people, but they must be used with discrimination. In an article in the *Modern Language Review* significantly entitled "Literature No 'Document' " Professor Elmer E. Stoll demonstrated that the brilliant comedies of Wycherley and Congreve are not to be taken as accurate mirrors of English life in the late seventeenth century. Then as now men and women did not go to the theater to see the dull details of their own monotonous lives enacted upon the stage. What they wanted was something strange and exciting; but, like a modern audience, they liked to have it presented with convincing verisimilitude in speech, manners, and dress. Many Northern and European and, I fear, Southern readers make the mistake of identifying Faulkner's fictitious Yoknapatawpha County with the actual state of Mississippi. It is quite possible that an informed historian could parallel nearly every character and incident in Faulkner's great cycle with some person or event in the history of the state; and yet Faulkner's world is as dark a literary domain as Thomas Hardy's Wessex and almost as remote from real life as the Poictesme of James Branch Cabell or the No Man's Land of Edgar Allan Poe.

If you want a complete literary picture of Mississippi life, you will find certain aspects of it well portrayed in writings by Joseph Glover Baldwin, William Gilmore Simms, Irwin Russell, George W. Cable, Stark Young, Richard Wright, William Faulkner, and Eudora Welty. After reading all these, if you persevere so long, you may be somewhat confused. Then you had better, if you want to understand the Mississippians, consult the findings of economists, sociologists, journalists, and historians; and you might do well to read whatever you can find of worth written by intelligent observers from outside the state. After that—or rather, long before—you had better go and observe Mississippi life with your own eyes. That life is as inexhaustible as the life of the London of Shakespeare or of Dickens or the Paris of Hugo and Balzac. There is no literary mirror which will reflect that life in all its infinite variety of character and incident.

We sometimes forget that until after the middle of the nineteenth century history was often regarded as a branch of literature. By the highest literary standards the works of Herodotus and Thucydides, of Livy and Tacitus belong to belles-lettres; so also do the historical works of Gibbon and Macaulay, of Prescott, Motley, and Parkman. For better or for worse nowadays the writing of history—whether in monographs, special studies, or textbooks—is largely in the hands of university professors and their graduate students. The gain in thoroughness and accuracy is very great, but there is a loss, too. The production of readable historical books is too often left to amateurs, journalists, or propagandists; and many of these are either biased or incompetent. Too few professors or graduate students—including those whose specialty is literature—can write well enough to interest a university press, much less a large commercial publishing house. One widely-used manual prepared for graduate students in history does suggest as an afterthought that when the student has collected his materials and written his thesis, he should devote a little time to polishing his style. No book written in that way can possibly have any merit as literature. Let me say, however, that in our time fortunately we have had historians who have written with skill and charm historical works of wide scope. I think immediately of Allan Nevins and of the late Carl Becker, and in England there is that forceful writer and man of many magnificent gifts, Sir Winston Churchill.

The first notable historical romancer, Sir Walter Scott, had a very great influence upon the writing of history, which up to his time in Britain had been too often concerned with few events outside of war and politics. In his essay on "History" Macaulay wrote:

At Lincoln Cathedral there is a beautiful painted window which was made by an apprentice out of the pieces of glass which had been rejected by his master. It is so far superior to every other in the church, that, according to the tradition, the vanquished artist killed himself from mortification. Sir Walter Scott, in the same manner, has used those fragments of truth which historians have scornfully thrown behind them in a manner which may well excite their envy. He has constructed out of their gleanings works which, even when considered as histories, are scarcely less valuable than theirs.

Anyone who has read the vivid description of London life in the late seventeenth century in Macaulay's *History of England* can hardly fail to note the influence of Scott. That influence is obvious also in the works of John Richard Green, of Prescott, Motley, and Charles Gayarré, the historian of Louisiana. One finds it also in the works of Francis Parkman though here there is also the stronger influence of James Fenimore Cooper. It was Parkman's reading of the Leather-Stocking Tales in his boyhood that gave him his vision of his life work, which he described as "the American conflict between France and England, or, in other words, the history of the American forest. . . ."

There are many so-called historical novels and fictionized biographies in which the historian finds bias, trivialities, or historical errors already exposed but still repeated from generation to generation. There are also historical novels in which the author has taken great pains to give us the correct details of dress and table manners but has interpolated a modern love story glaringly out of keeping with all that is known of the relations between the sexes in ancient Greece or Rome or Palestine. William Gilmore Simms, who in his six Revolutionary Romances did his best to keep the historical record straight, must have been greatly pleased by the tribute paid him one hundred years ago in a Charleston address delivered by Prescott, the New England historian:

> I cannot refer to [the American Revolution] without acknowledging the debt which I think the State owes to one of her most distinguished sons, for the fidelity with which he has preserved its memory, the vigor and beauty with which he has painted its most stirring scenes, and kept alive in fiction the portraits of its most famous heroes.

In the Preface to his *Life and Labor in the Old South* the late Ulrich B. Phillips praised the historical insight that Stephen Vincent Benét displayed in his *John Brown's Body,* which might be described as a historical romance in verse. Phillips seemed a little envious. The poet, the dramatist, and the novelist make it all look so easy. Why should they trouble themselves about bibliographies, footnotes, or even original sources? They fill in lacunae for which there is little or no specific evidence, drawing upon the imagination for telling details or dramatic scenes.

The gifted novelist has the power to make us see and hear, to make us imaginatively experience for ourselves events which took place centuries before we were born. The story of the Confederacy has been exceptionally well told in our time by Professor E. Merton Coulter and Colonel Robert S. Henry; and yet when someone mentions the approaching centennial of the Civil War, where do our mental images of that conflict come from? In my youth one's conception of the Civil War was formed largely by Cooke's *Surry of Eagle's Nest,* Mary Johnston's *The Long Roll,* Ellen Glasgow's *The Battle-Ground,* and Stephen Crane's *The Red Badge of Courage.* Since 1936, however, when one thinks of the war in Georgia, the scenes that come most vividly to mind derive from *Gone With the Wind,* either the novel or the motion picture or from both.

As one whose special interest is in American literature, I wish that our historians had a keener interest in the fringes of legend and myth that gather around important historical figures and events. Dixon Wecter and Gerald Johnson have published provocative studies of American heroes and hero-worship, but they tell us little about the process by which historical personages are transformed—and often distorted—into symbols. Clouds of stories akin to folklore cluster about Captain John Smith and Pocahontas, David Crockett and John Brown, George Washington and Abraham Lincoln. For too many of us these very real human beings have become nothing but figureheads or plaster saints. And yet as symbols they have had much to do with establishing our national tradition. They have helped to give us a unity of feeling and to make us feel that ours is a country worth fighting for.

If you want full information about the legends that have obscured or simplified the complex personality of George Washington, you will not find it in Douglas Southall Freeman's monumental biography. Freeman was relying only upon first-hand materials. If you are interested in Parson Weems's story of little George's hatchet and the cherry tree, you should look into the late William Alfred Bryan's *George Washington in Literature.* This study, I may say, was written as a doctor's dissertation by a friend and student of mine who died just two weeks before the day set for his final examination. If you are interested in the literary role of Lincoln, you will consult *The Lincoln Legend,* written by another friend and former student, Roy P. Basler, whose dissertation is so far as I know the only one ever recommended by The Book-of-the-Month Club.

One historian, Wilbur Cortez Abbott of Yale University, has traced the development of Oliver Cromwell's reputation down to the time of his rehabilitation in the nineteenth century. Yet in his *Conflicts with Oblivion* (1924) Professor Abbott showed no interest in legends or in Cromwell's literary role. Nor did he reveal any awareness that Cromwell's reputation was intimately bound up with the changing conception of the Puritans. The New England Puritans as we find them portrayed in *The Scarlet Letter* represent a complex legendary development covering two centuries on both sides of the Atlantic. Involved in it are Samuel Butler's *Hudibras,* which satirized the Puritans; Scott's *Woodstock,* which included an ugly portrait of Cromwell; and in this country numerous New England chronicles, of which the most notable is Cotton Mather's huge *Magnalia Christi Americana.* All of these, aided by failing memories and a sequence of events which brought about a new attitude toward the receding past had a part in the transformation of the historical Puritans, who were of many kinds, into a single type, the strong, stern, and humorless type best represented by the historical Captain John Endicott, who plays a leading part in "The Maypole of Merry Mount" and "Endicott and the Red Cross." The gentler and more lovable Puritans and Pilgrims represented by John Winthrop and William Bradford did not fit into Hawthorne's fictional pattern. Even today in spite of the numerous attempts of history teachers in classrooms and in textbooks to correct the traditional picture, it is difficult for us to believe that Puritan men and women loved beautiful clothes and good music and had a sense of humor.

A century after Hawthorne's time it is difficult for us to understand how barren and unromantic the brief American past seemed to him and his contemporaries. In the Preface to *The Marble Faun,* for the setting of which Hawthorne had gone to Italy, he complained of "the difficulty of writing a romance about a country [meaning the United States] where there is no shadow, no antiquity, no mystery, no picturesque and gloomy wrong, nor anything but a commonplace prosperity, in broad and simple daylight, as is happily the case with my dear native land." We know now that our American heritage of folklore and legend is much richer than the great New Englanders ever dreamed; and yet there is no denying the fact that the great literary legends of the world arose in primitive times when there were no historians but the poets. Horace reminded his Roman readers that doubtless there were heroes before Agamemnon; but as Alexander Pope in an imitation of Horace wrote:

> Vain was the chief's, the sage's pride!
> They had no poet, and they died.

Homer no doubt found the story of the siege of Troy highly developed when it came into his hands. The folk imagination of the gifted Greeks had been at work upon it for several generations. Another example is that belated offshoot of the Troy cycle, the story of Troilus and Cressida. This story, which is not to be found in Homer or Vergil, grew up in the centuries when few men in Western Europe could read Latin and almost no one read Homer's Greek; and it received memorable treatment at the hands of Boccaccio, Chaucer, and Shakespeare. The Dark Ages also gave us the finest of all the later European legends, the cycle of King Arthur and the Knights of the Round Table. That rich aggregation of legendary materials developed before there were any printing presses or professors of history who made it their business to keep the record straight.

Americans are, I am certain, as highly imaginative and probably as much given to the creation of legends as other peoples, but our history is too recent and too well known for us to have accumulated such a literary treasury of legend, myth, and folklore as one finds, for example, in the Lowland Scotland of Burns and Scott. In my study of the literary role of Pocahontas and Captain John Smith I ventured the suggestion that if Virginia had been settled in the "dark backward and abysm of time" when the Arthurian cycle was slowly taking shape, we might today have the fully developed national epic story of a gallant Knight of the Round Table who after an adventurous career with Lancelot and Bedivere came to Virginia, married an Indian princess, and became the venerable ancestor of the great Virginia soldiers and statesmen of the Revolution. Captain John Smith, that middle-class soldier of fortune, would be our Aeneas, who brought an ancient civilization to a new world. Pocahontas would of course be the American counterpart of Lavinia, the Italian princess who married Aeneas. But here sober pedestrian fact prevailed over the legend-making faculty: Smith, the confirmed bachelor, left the princess and went back to England, and Pocahontas became the second wife of that unromantic tobacco farmer, John Rolfe. Nevertheless, Pocahontas became one of our most beautiful symbols and she is so represented in Vachel Lindsay's "Our Mother Pocahontas" and Hart Crane's "Brooklyn Bridge."

Only the specialist will take the time to make himself familiar with every aspect of the career of a great man like Washington or Lincoln. As time recedes, the people, if they remember the man at all, convert him into a symbol of something they can cherish. And thus, as Emerson wrote in his essay on "History":

> Time dissipates to shining ether the solid angularity of facts. No anchor, no cable, no fences avail to keep a fact a fact. Babylon, Troy, Tyre, Palestine and even early Rome are passing already into fiction. . . . Who cares what the fact was when we have thus made a constellation of it to hang in heaven an immortal sign? London and Paris and New York must go the same way. "What is History," said Napoleon, "but a fable agreed upon?"

The historian may find Emerson's seeming lack of regard for fact deplorable; but the student of literature is likely to agree with Emerson, for he is fascinated by literary symbols and sees them as indispensable. Indeed, in our time literary critics are so preoccupied with symbols that some of them seem to me engaged in a guessing game. If T. S. Eliot and William Faulkner ever take the trouble to explain their use of symbols, they may highly embarrass a large number of living scholars who have written critical articles about their writings.

No true historian would ever join in Emerson's sweeping pronouncement that it doesn't matter what the actual fact was when we have found a symbolic use for it. That would be to abrogate his function as historian; namely, to search out and to publish a true account unadorned by legend or myth. In his Preface to *Myths and Men* Professor Bernard Mayo, speaking of Washington, Henry, and Jefferson, expressed the point of view of the true historian: "All three [of these case histories in hero-worship] reveal how the flesh-and-blood men, humanly fallible yet with inspiring qualities of greatness, have been distorted and obscured by conflicting interpretations and by myths that defame and myths that glorify."

I could wish that some of our twentieth-century writers of fiction had the high regard for the actual fact that seems basic to the scientist and the historian. Many of our literary expatriates who in the 1920's lived in Paris saw their native land as the least civilized country in the world. In Paris they discovered Emile Zola and that brand of extreme literary realism which is called naturalism. Debunking was the literary fashion in Greenwich Village as well as on the Left Bank of the Seine. Many of our literary rebels had no faith in democracy and no use for the American tradition, whether in literature or in politics. In the 1930's when the Great Depression was at its height many writers who had hitherto shown no interest in political theory suddenly discovered Marx and Lenin and were tremendously impressed by what they read about the Communist regime in Russia. Other writers, including Ezra Pound, embraced a Fascist or a Nazi ideology. Most of these writers were destined to be disillusioned by a rapid and momentous sequence of events: the *Anschluss* with Austria, appeasement at Munich, the rape of Czechoslovakia, the Hitler-Stalin Pact of 1939, the invasion of Poland, and the attack on Pearl Harbor. Our writers, like so many other Americans, had to learn the hard way that American democracy with all its imperfections in practice is yet something very precious that we must be prepared to fight for and, if need be, give our lives to preserve for our children and grandchildren.

Let me make it clear that I would not deny to the

novelist the right to depict and condemn the ugly aspects of American life. That right is fundamental, and we should be grateful to Cooper, Melville, Mark Twain, Sinclair Lewis, and others for the use they have made of it. Nevertheless, I find the situation profoundly disturbing. At the very time that the United States was fast becoming the chief champion of democracy and the rights of man in a world divided between the Free World and Communist countries beyond the Iron Curtain we find that many of our ablest writers have unwittingly furnished propaganda for the Fascists, the Nazis, and the Communists. The situation does not speak well for the political intelligence of our novelists.

We Americans are a naive people. We expect other nations to like and admire us when we continually point out our national shortcomings. We habitually wash our dirty linen in public and hang it out to dry, so to speak, on the international line where all the world may see it—and yet we are chagrined when we find ourselves slandered and disliked in both hemispheres. We discover too late that giving away our tax dollars by the million does not make foreigners love us, either. Last spring some Americans who should have known better selected for exhibition in Moscow books and pictures which, so it seemed to President Eisenhower and most other Americans, misrepresented the lives and the ideals of the American people. The Communists do not make that mistake.

In recent years many American professors and students lecturing or studying in foreign universities have discovered what was forcefully brought home to me first in Vienna and later in Athens; namely, that much anti-American sentiment in the world of today can be traced to reading American fiction and seeing American motion pictures. The European intellectual has inherited many age-old misconceptions of American life, and he seldom has any first-hand knowledge of life in this country. And so when he reads *An American Tragedy, Babbitt* or *Main Street, The Grapes of Wrath, Tobacco Road, Uncle Tom's Children, Desire Under the Elms, Studs Lonigan, Manhattan Transfer,* or *The Sound and the Fury,* he takes them as literally accurate transcripts of American life. What wonder if he concludes that we are underneath a thin veneer the least civilized nation in the Western world and that life in the United States—and especially in the South—is the life of a savage people? Is it any wonder that the German and the Japanese war lords came to the conclusion that Americans were degenerate and would not prove formidable enemies in war?

In the period between the two World Wars when so many of our best novels and short stories were being written, the totalitarian countries were not only very busy with their vicious propaganda about us; they were at the same time re-writing the histories of their own countries in order to show that all of Europe's great men belonged to the Nordic race or else that all the great inventions and scientific discoveries were made by Russians.

Yet the Communist party line has been changed so often that one wonders how any intelligent person behind the Iron Curtain can possibly believe any official Russian pronouncement. When we consider the periodic and unscrupulous re-writing of Russian history which goes on in the Kremlin, is it any wonder that the Soviet hierarchy was alarmed by Boris Pasternak's *Doctor Zhivago*? In this powerful novel we have a vivid historical panorama of Russian history from 1905 until after the Second World War. It is the work of a profoundly religious poet who had hoped much from the Russian Revolution in 1917. *Doctor Zhivago* is a shocking story of Communist inefficiency, selfishness, unbelief, moral decay, hatred, and betrayal of decent ideals. If the Russians were permitted to read the novel, they might recognize the book as an authentic history and come to share the disillusionment of Lara, Antipov, Tonia, and Doctor Zhivago himself.

Many of the novels written about the South have come from Northern and English writers, and thus our section is almost unique in that fiction depicting life in the Southern states represents two long-established and widely differing traditions. In modern times these have become so blended and confused that when you read a new Southern novel, whether written by a Southerner or a Northerner, you are likely in one chapter to be reminded of Joel Chandler Harris or Thomas Nelson Page and in the next chapter you may find an echo of *Uncle Tom's Cabin* or *Miss Ravenel's Conversion from Secession to Loyalty*. The Abolitionists, most of whom were never south of the Ohio or the Potomac, built up a legend of the South as a semi-barbarous region inhabited only by an oligarchy of rich and cruel planters, thousands of overworked and terribly abused Negro slaves, and hundreds of poor-whites, the evil by-product of the slave system. The Abolitionists apparently never looked into the census reports and they ignored the millions of Southern yeomen who, if they owned any slaves, worked in the cotton and tobacco fields beside them from sun-up till sun-down. So powerful was this Abolitionist myth of a semi-barbarous South that eventually it imposed itself upon intelligent Northern men who had spent months or years in the South and should have known better. Among them were Dr. William Ellery Channing, the great Unitarian divine, who as a young man spent eighteen months as a tutor in Richmond; Amos Bronson Alcott, the Concord philosopher and schoolmaster, who spent four years as a peddler in Virginia and the Carolinas; and Ralph Waldo Emerson, who as a young man spent a winter in South Carolina and Florida. Franklin D. Roosevelt once referred to the South as the nation's No. 1 Economic Problem. He might have noted that for something over a century our section had been looked upon in the North as the nation's No. 1 Moral Problem.

It is generally conceded that a majority of the best American writers of our time are Southerners; it is also generally recognized that the richest veins of literary materials in this country are in the Southern states; and yet paradoxically the South long has been and still is subject to greater misrepresentation in fiction than any other section. In his Lamar Lectures two years ago Donald Davidson discussed this unhealthy situation, and I do not need to say much about it. In July of the very same year an associate editor of the *American Mercury* published an article entitled "Why Pick on Dixie?" in which he noted what seemed to him a "new and wonder formula for literary success." "Damn the South" is of course no new formula. Nor was it new when some twenty years ago Clare Boothe Luce wrote the popular play, *Kiss the Boys Good-bye,* in which she ridiculed a number of Southern ways. In the preface to the published play she made the astonishing assertion: "We are not, perhaps, sufficiently aware that 'Southernism' is a particular and highly matured form of Fascism with which America has lived more or less peacefully for seventy-five years."

That kind of slander coming from an outsider does not greatly disturb me. What is really disheartening is to find a native Southerner, like Erskine Caldwell, playing up the old Abolitionist legend of a barbarous South. No literary critic would fail to note such distortion of fact in a book written by a journalist, a sociologist, an economist, or a historian. Why should the author of *Tobacco Road* be permitted to claim exemption from such criticism because it is in the domain of belles-lettres? Some years ago after class I had an argument on this very point with a graduate student for whom at that time William Faulkner was the greatest of all American novelists. He argued that since the literary movement we call naturalism had arrived in America, no one had a right to criticize the authors of *Sanctuary* and *Tobacco Road* for deliberately putting into their books what they knew would shock Mississippians and Georgians and furnish materials for Nazi and Communist propaganda. In defending my position I might have quoted from Faulkner's introduction to a later edition of his novel: "To me this is a cheap idea because it was deliberately conceived to make money." Ellen Glasgow, who quotes this sentence in one of her letters, comments:

> That covers a good deal of that kind of writing nowadays in the South. If anything is too vile and too degenerate to exist anywhere else it is assigned to the "honest" school of Southern fiction, and swallowed whole, bait and all, by Northern readers, who have never been below Washington, but have a strong appetite.

There is also a Southern literary legend which pictures a Golden Age in the slaveholding South. Now the remarkable thing about this legend is that apart from the poor-whites it plays up the very same classes as the

Northern legend: the great planters and the Negro slaves. Like the Northern legend, it practically ignores some four million yeomen farmers. They did not belong to the First Families. No wonder that it took so long for Southern historians to re-discover these millions of the people whom the late Frank Owsley called "the plain folk of the South." In the 1880's and 1890's the Southern legend of the Old South as embodied in *Nights with Uncle Remus* and *In Ole Virginia* enjoyed an enormous vogue in the North. Something of the charm of the legend survives in Stark Young's *So Red the Rose* and Margaret Mitchell's best-seller, *Gone With the Wind*. Nowadays, however, the South is the conventional background for Gothic horrors, and favorite characters are poor-whites, perverts, and the most primitive types of both whites and blacks. If there are any aristocrats around, they are sure to be degenerates.

Southern literature, one must always bear in mind, is produced primarily for the export trade. Since the publishers, the magazine editors, and the great majority of those who buy books and magazines live outside the South, the demand is often for the kind of fiction which, it seems to most Southerners, misrepresents our way of life. But whether Southern readers like the commercial product is not a matter of prime importance in a publisher's eyes. Under these circumstances the temptation confronting the Southern writer to give his readers a distorted picture of the life of his own people is very great.

And yet our own unreal legend of Southern life may be a great handicap to the novelist who does not want to displease his Southern readers. Fortunately in the twentieth century the South has the fine novels of Ellen Glasgow, Thomas Wolfe, DuBose Heyward, Julia Peterkin, Eudora Welty, and many others, honest and clear-sighted writers who have corrected many mistaken notions of the South and given us memorable pictures of people and places not adequately recorded by their predecessors.

Most of the emphasis in these lectures, however, will be upon the nineteenth century. That happens to be the period which I know best, but there is another reason for my emphasis upon it: Everybody knows about the Southern Renaissance, and yet many persons seem to assume that until after the First World War the South had produced no literature of importance. Yet it ought to be obvious to every student of literature and history that one cannot fully understand the age in which we live without a working knowledge of the nineteenth century. Much of what I shall say will deal with Virginia and Georgia. In my lecture on Virginia I shall speak chiefly of the gentlemen planters; in speaking of Georgia I shall emphasize other classes. I hope none of you will conclude that I do not know that there were Southern gentlemen and ladies in this state and that Virginia had its share of second families and poor-whites.

LECTURE
TWO

Virginia Life in Fiction

IT IS DIFFICULT FOR A MODERN AMERICAN TO PICTURE Jamestown Island or Plymouth Harbor as the first settlers actually saw them. Neither the Pilgrim Fathers nor the Virginian settlers thought of themselves as the founders of a great state in a new nation which twice in the twentieth century would come to the rescue of little England in a time of great peril. We see the pioneers through a mistlike accumulation of history, legend, and patriotic sentiment which makes William Bradford and Captain John Smith seem larger than human.

Among the settlers bound for Virginia some of the better-educated had perhaps read the fine "Ode to the Virginian Voyage," in which Michael Drayton had bidden them bon voyage and farewell. I quote the first and the fourth stanzas.

> You brave Heroique minds,
> Worthy your Countries Name;
> That Honour still pursue,
> Goe, and subdue,
> Whilst loyt'ring Hinds
> Lurke here at home, with shame.

And cheerefully at Sea,
Successe you still intice,
    To get the Pearle and Gold,
    And ours to hold,
VIRGINIA,
Earth's onely Paradise.

The gentlemen adventurers who expected to find gold on the banks of the James were doomed to disappointment. It was not in gold nuggets or in pearls but in the lowly tobacco plant that fortunes were to be made in Virginia. Among the settlers there were fortunately a few natural-born frontiersmen like Captain John Smith, who loved the new land from the first. That land, however, held deadly perils for the newcomers, and disease and hostile Indians took as heavy a toll in Virginia as in New England. For homesick Englishmen stricken with malaria and expecting an Indian attack on the hot and humid banks of the James the primeval Virginian forest must have seemed an unkindly, unhomely land as different as possible from rural England. It was to be many years before the Virginians ceased referring to England as "home."

We love best the kind of landscape in which our early years were spent, and it is always difficult for us to learn to feel at home where all is strange. The Scotch-Irish immigrants who in the early eighteenth century began pouring into the Shenandoah Valley settled mainly in the hill country which reminded them of the landscape they had known in Scotland or northern Ireland. The shrewd German settlers coming from the flat country of the lower Rhine made for the rich meadow lands along the Virginia rivers. The Virginians came to love their land after they and their fathers had worked and fought for it. For Robert Beverley, writing in 1705, Virginia was "my Country," and he could not bear to hear it abused. It was the gross English misrepresentation of the life of his own people that moved Beverley "in Justice [as he says] to so fine a Country," to undertake his *History and Present State of Virginia.*

On Phi Beta Kappa Day at William and Mary College, December 5, 1941, Robert Frost read a beautiful poem entitled "The Gift Outright," in which he tells us just how it was that the descendants of the English settlers finally became Virginians and Americans. "The land was ours before we were the land's," as the poet phrased it; and for many years "we were England's, still colonials." The change came when we finally gave ourselves unreservedly to the land we were living in.

> Such as we were we gave ourselves outright
> (The deed of gifts was many deeds of war)
> To the land vaguely realizing westward,
> But still unstoried, artless, unenhanced,
> Such as she was, such as she would become.

"The deed of gift," as Frost puts it, "was many deeds of war." The Virginians loved the land for which again and again they had fought the Indians as they were later to fight the French and the English and finally and most desperately the invading Union armies. A. E. Housman might have been thinking of many young Virginians or Georgians when he wrote the memorable four-line poem:

> Here dead lie we because we did not choose
> To live and shame the land from which we sprung.
> Life, to be sure, is nothing much to lose,
> But young men think it is, and we were young.

The Virginians loved their land passionately. The

defect of their devotion was a certain provincial complacency which led them to look down upon those who lived in less fortunate regions. The Reverend Hugh Jones, who in 1724 published *The Present State of Virginia,* put it this way:

> If *New England* be called a Receptacle of Dissenters, and [New York] an *Amsterdam* of Religion, *Pensylvania* the Nursery of Quakers, *Maryland* the Retirement of *Roman Catholics, North Carolina* the Refuge of Run-aways, and *South Carolina* the Delight of Buccaneers and Pyrates, *Virginia* may be justly esteemed the happy Retreat of *true Britons* and *true Churchmen.* . . .

If the colony of Georgia had been in existence in 1724, it would probably have fared no better in Jones's book than the Carolinas.

For us that have three and a half centuries of eventful history to look back upon in the Old Dominion, that state now seems as rich as any of the fifty states in heroic deeds, myths, legends, and in places where memorable events occurred. In 1607, however, Virginia was, in the words of Robert Frost, "still unstoried, artless, unenhanced." How did the change come about? Our writers—and not all of them were Virginians or even Americans—had something to do with the change; but the writers did not create the rich literary materials which they used. The writers had the eyes to see and the technical skill needed to exploit them, but the Virginians themselves supplied the materials.

It was a long time before the brief American past acquired that romantic aura of history and legend which attracts the poet and the novelist. These associations and the legends that developed along with them were in large part the creation of the popular imagination. In a sense somewhat different from what Herder had in mind when he said: *"Das Volk dichtet"* we may speak of the creative function of the folk imagination. When some two centuries after the founding of Jamestown our first novelists turned their attention to American life, they discovered ready to hand the rich materials which Carl Van Doren called the three "Matters of American Romance": the period of settlement, the frontier, and the American Revolution. Young American writers of talent like Cooper, Hawthorne, Kennedy, and Simms, full of admiration for Scott's historical romances, found in them a suitable technique for handling American materials. And thus certain sections of the new land ceased to be "unstoried, artless, unenhanced."

The achievement of their political independence prompted Americans to take a new look at the history of their country, and they found in it something new and highly significant. Captain John Smith and Pocahontas were now to be reckoned among the founders of a great state if indeed not of a great nation. The rebel Nathaniel Bacon was now seen as a forerunner of George Washington fighting a war for independence just a century too soon. A romantic halo settled over the heads of frontier explorers and Indian fighters, especially Daniel Boone and David Crockett. As the last of the hostile Indians were pushed westward over the Appalachians, Americans along the seaboard began to feel keenly the pathos of the red man's fate, and the Indian was hailed as a unique figure, one in which the Old World had no share. In the popular imagination the American Revolution loomed up as a heroic age with heroes and villains contending for an empire far larger than the British Isles. Actually the Revolution had been a very unpleasant civil war, but complicated issues became simplified. Lord North, George III, and Benedict Arnold became villains without redeeming traits. And as the glamour gathered over the leading statesmen and soldiers who saw the long struggle through, they began to look larger and more nearly perfect than one expects of ordinary mankind. George Washington, who had played so large a part in winning the war and in making a nation out of thirteen divergent states, became the chief symbol of the new nation. In his case, however, the worshipful attitude of Americans long made it difficult for any writer to picture him as anything but a plaster saint, a prig, or a hollow emblem of Americanism.

Southerners, and especially Virginians, are—or used to be—much given to disparaging the present and idealizing the past. I think of an old farmer who once said to me in all seriousness that the sap in the sugar maple tree was not as sweet as it was when he was a boy. Even the ex-slaves idealized the past. You may remember Mark Twain's story of an old Negro woman who, hearing a Northern visitor praise the beauty of a Southern moonlight night, said with a shake of her head: "Ah, bless yo' heart, honey; you jes' ought to seen dat moon befo' de waw!" For Negroes as well as whites the years which followed the Civil War, like those which had followed the American Revolution, were difficult years. No wonder that both whites and blacks looked back longingly to the years before the war when no one went hungry or lacked a home of some kind.

In January, 1919, while still in uniform I went back to Columbia University to write a doctor's dissertation on "Virginia Life in Fiction." I quickly discovered that I was almost as much concerned with history as with fiction. Carl Van Doren, then a young instructor, read my dissertation chapter by chapter as I wrote it, and remarked that it seemed to him that the remote Virginian past was buried under as many layers of legend as the numerous strata which Heinrich Schliemann found overlying Homer's Troy. In those days I had something of the skeptical outlook of the Young Intellectuals of the 1920's, most of whom had no interest in the past. I was by no means without pride in my native state, but I found amusement in tracing the development to huge proportions of the Cavalier legend which made most Virginians and indeed ultimately all Southerners descendants of the British gentry, sometimes of the British nobility. I learned from the historians that among the Cavaliers who followed the fortunes of Charles I there were thousands of men who were not in the social sense gentlemen. I found also that while the number of Cavalier gentlemen who settled in Virginia was fewer than represented in the legend, the number of indentured servants who came to Virginia was much larger than Virginians liked to admit.

There were, however, some English gentlemen among the Cavaliers who settled in Virginia; and, as John Spencer Bassett has pointed out, "they had an influence out of proportion to their numbers. They gave manners a warmer tone; they emphasized the ideal of country life; they gave Virginians their passion for handsome houses and fast horses; and they gave public life something more than it had before of the English notion that offices should be held for the benefit of the gentry." The Virginian aristocracy, like that of South Carolina or Massachusetts, was largely home-grown; but much the same could be said of the English aristocracy. It was never quite a closed circle. In Virginia men of ability managed in various ways to win offices and land for themselves or for their children. There was a saying in Virginia that it takes three generations to make a gentleman and four to make a lady. The Virginians were particular about their wives and daughters.

The South's finest product, as we often fail to remember, was not its cotton or tobacco or its textile and cigarette factories or even its literature, but its men and women. In the period of the Revolution Virginia gave the nation the most remarkable group of great men—soldiers and statesmen—that this country has yet produced. George Washington, Thomas Jefferson, Arthur and Richard Henry Lee—like William Byrd before them and Robert E. Lee after them—were gentlemen; and if we would understand them, we must remember that the term "gentleman," more or less meaningless now—unless you place a negative in front of it—stood for a fine ideal. That ideal is out of fashion, especially, it would seem, among Southern writers of fiction. C. P. Lee has shown what a sorry role the gentleman plays in twentieth-century Southern fiction. One might almost say that the Southern novelist wishes that the last surviving Southern gentleman would, like Robinson's Richard Cory, who was "a gentleman from sole to crown," go home "and put a bullet through his head." Yet what so many of our young people most admire is hardly a worthy substitute for men like Lee and Washington. We admire the "power elite," executives with lavish expense accounts, yachts, and Cadillacs, the star athletes, and above all, I fear, the numerous show people in and outside of Hollywood who in recent years have built themselves up as the great American aristocracy.

The gentlemanly ideal was fading in England in the

time of Lord Chesterfield, of whose once famous letters Samuel Johnson remarked too severely that they taught the manners of a dancing master and the morals of a whore. In 1850 Tennyson wrote in *In Memoriam* of his friend Arthur Hallam:

> And thus he bore without abuse
> The grand old name of gentleman,
> Defamed by every charlatan,
> And soil'd with all ignoble use.

Charles Eliot Norton, the friend of Lowell, Emerson, and Carlyle, is reputed to have said to his class in Fine Arts at Harvard some time before his retirement in 1898: "I don't suppose any of you young men ever saw a gentleman." Norton, I am sure, was mistaken. There were some fine New England gentlemen in the Harvard faculty when I was a student there after Norton's time; and in the faculty of little Richmond College, when I was an undergraduate, there were gentlemen altogether worthy of their Virginian heritage. I have known no finer gentlemen than Dean Le Baron Russell Briggs of Harvard and President Frederick William Boatwright of what is now the University of Richmond. Each of these men had "the mingled expression of intelligence and benignity" which was for Joseph Glover Baldwin above all other marks "the unmistakable, uncounterfeitable outward sign of a true gentleman."

The gentlemanly ideal is an ancient one. Achilles, Ulysses, and Aeneas were, like David and Jonathan, gentlemen of a kind; but it was left to the age of chivalry to give the old ideal a new meaning. The chivalric ideal is beautifully set forth in Tennyson's "Guenevere" when King Arthur describes the oath taken by his Knights of the Round Table:

> I made them lay their hands in mine and swear
> To reverence the King, as if he were
> Their conscience, and their conscience as their King,
> To break the heathen and uphold the Christ,
> To ride abroad redressing human wrongs,
> To speak no slander, no, nor listen to it,
> To honour his own word as if his God's,
> To lead sweet lives in purest chastity;
> To love one maiden only, cleave to her,
> And worship her by years of noble deeds,
> Until they won her; for indeed I knew
> Of no more subtle master under heaven
> Than is a maiden passion for a maid,
> Not only to keep down the base in man,
> But teach high thought, and amiable words
> And courtliness, and the desire of fame,
> And love of truth, and all that makes a man.

Among the most memorable portraits in Chaucer's Prologue to *The Canterbury Tales* is that of the "verray parfit gentil knight"

> That fro the tyme that he first began
> To ryden out, he loved chivalrye,
> Trouthe and Honour, fredom and curteisye.

Here, as in "Guenevere," we have the ideal of the Happy Warrior with Christian overtones; and they are certainly evident in such gentlemen as Robert E. Lee and Sidney Lanier. I think of Saint Paul's exhortation to the Philippians: "Finally, brethren, whatsoever things are true, whatsoever things are honest, whatsoever things are just, whatsoever things are pure, whatsoever things are lovely, whatsoever things are of good report; if there be any virtue, and if there be any praise, think on these things." The Christian ideal has its part in Spenser's *The Faerie Queene,* of which the poet said: "The generall end therefore of all the booke is to fashion a gentleman or noble person in vertuous and gentle discipline. . . ." Another Elizabethan poet, Thomas Dekker, wrote the memorable lines which characterize a gentleman born in Nazareth nearly two thousand years ago:

> The best of men
> That ere wore earth about him, was a sufferer,
> A soft, meek, patient, humble, tranquil spirit,
> The first true gentleman that ever breath'd.

The Christian element, however, was too often absent or rarely seen. King Charles II is said to have remarked that Presbyterianism was not a religion for gentlemen. Nor would King Charles, if he knew anything about a Baptist preacher by the name of Bunyan, writing *The Pilgrim's Progress* in Bedford Jail, have regarded this tinker's son as in any sense a gentleman. But Bunyan's Captain Great-heart, Christiana's guide, is a finer gentleman than the witty King Charles. Today a pessimistic observer, noting how the ideal once suggested by the phrase "Christian gentleman" has faded, might quote from George Santayana's *The Genteel Tradition*: ". . . the gist of modern history would seem to be this: a many-sided insurrection of the unregenerate natural man, with all his physical powers and affinities, against the regimen of Christendom."

The Virginia planters, whether or not of gentle blood, tried as best they could to live on their farms like the country gentlemen of rural England. Let me read you a portion of a description of an eighteenth-century English gentleman written by his daughter, who was a native of Virginia:

> He gave the best example, the best advice, the most bounteous hospitality to his friends; the tenderest care to his dependents. . . . He was never familiar, though perfectly simple and natural; he was the same with the meanest man

as with the greatest, and as courteous to a black slave-girl as to the Governor's wife. No one ever thought of taking a liberty with him (except once a tipsy gentleman from York. . . .) . . . . His courtesy was not put on like a Sunday suit and laid by when the company went away. . . . They say he liked to be the first in his company; but what company was there in which he would not be first?

That is from Thackeray's description of Henry Esmond, who, you may remember, married Lady Castlewood and settled in Westmoreland County as a friend and neighbor of George Washington. When he wrote this passage, Thackeray had not yet visited this country. When he did, he found Virginians more like his own people in England than Americans in other states.

Of that Virginia gentleman who was "first in war, first in peace, and first in the hearts of his countrymen" Thomas Jefferson in 1814 wrote in a memorable letter to Walter Jones:

His integrity was most pure, his justice the most inflexible I have ever known, no motives of interest or consanguinity, of friendship or hatred, being able to bias his decision. He was, indeed, in every sense of the words, a wise, a good, and a great man. . . . His person, you know, was fine, his stature exactly what one would wish, his deportment easy, erect and noble; the best horseman of his age, and the most graceful figure that could be seen on horseback. . . . On the whole, his character was, in its mass, perfect, in nothing bad, in few points indifferent; and it may truly be said, that never did nature and fortune combine more perfectly to make a man great, and to place him in the same constellation with whatever worthies have merited from man an everlasting remembrance.

Washington deserved to the full the fine tribute which Lowell in 1875 paid him in "Under the Old Elm," in which the New England poet held out the hand of reconciliation to the defeated South:

> Virginia gave us this imperial man. . . .
> She gave us this unblemished gentleman. . . .
> Mother of States and undiminished men,
> Thou gavest us a country, giving him. . . .

Let us take as a more typical example of the Virginia planter-statesman that notable farmer and political scientist, John Taylor of Caroline. Thomas Hart Benton, who served with Taylor in the United States Senate, spoke of him as "the ideal of a republican statesman":

> . . . plain and solid, a wise counsellor, a ready and vigorous debater, acute and comprehensive, ripe in all historical and political knowledge, innately republican [democratic]—modest, courteous, benevolent, hospitable—a skilful, practical farmer, giving his time to his farm and his books, when not called by an emergency to the public service—and returning to his books and his farm when the emergency was over.

This generation finds it difficult to believe that, like Taylor, George Washington and Thomas Jefferson really preferred life on their farms to life in any city on the continent.

One of Taylor's contemporaries, John Randolph of Roanoke, in his letters to a nephew wrote:

> Do not . . . undervalue . . . the character of the *real* gentleman, which is the most respectable amongst men. It consists not of plate, and equipage, and rich living, . . . but in *truth,* courtesy, bravery, generosity, and learning, which last, although not *essential* to it, yet does very much to adorn and illustrate the character of the true gentleman. . . . Lay down this as a principle, that *truth* is to the other virtues, what vital air is to the human system.

Other gentlemanly qualities were a keen sense of honor, of decorum, justice, loyalty, and the spirit of public service. One might almost sum up the Elizabethan ideal in the one word "Magnanimity," best exemplified in Sir Philip Sidney. That ideal was still strong in Virginia during Jefferson's Presidency when John Davis, an English writer who spent many years in the state, wrote: "The higher Virginians seem to venerate themselves as men."

In 1949 a Northern scholar, Edwin H. Cady, published *The Gentleman in America: A Literary Study in American Culture,* in which he devoted only a single chapter to the South, and that chapter dealt chiefly with Thomas Jefferson. Of Jefferson's ideal of the gentleman he said: ". . . it is the Southern gentleman: an excellent blend of the Christian and Chesterfieldian ideals." Cady saw in Jefferson and Lee something of "the magnanimity of the Renaissance, and always a touch of the grace of the fine gentleman." Yet he could find almost nothing that distinguished the American gentleman in the South from his brother in the North, and he added: "This suggests that the American gentleman in the South was (and is) a magnificent figure; but that 'the Southern gentleman' is a genteel tradition." I suspect that Dr. Cady, like other Northern scholars whom I could name, found that research in the field of Southern culture offered more difficulties than research in New York and New England and so decided to neglect the South of the later nineteenth century. There can be no question that, in spite of the genteel tradition, the gentlemanly ideal retained its force in the conservative South longer than in the industrial North.

The Virginia planter families prided themselves in

being of gentle blood. The influence of their Cavalier blood, when they inherited any, may be disregarded; but their belief in their aristocratic heritage was profoundly influential. They had an ideal to live up to. The Southern gentleman was an aristocrat; and his leisure was based upon inherited property or money, good management, and generally upon the labor of Negro slaves. If pressed hard to defend his status in society, the planter might quote Burke or Aristotle, appeal to the Old or the New Testament, or in the last resort take the position taken by Senator James H. Hammond of South Carolina:

> In all social systems there must be a class to do the menial duties, to perform the drudgery of life. . . . It constitutes the very mudsill of society and of political government, and you might as well attempt to build a house in the air as to build either the one or the other, except on this mudsill.

The "mudsill" theory was peculiarly repugnant to Abraham Lincoln, our most notable example of the self-made American; but Senator Hammond no doubt seemed to many of his Southern contemporaries a realist who had the courage to face up to the unpleasant facts of life. In contemporary industrial America we have a very different economic goal: to raise the living standard of the common man, white and black, to the point where it will compare not unfavorably with that of the well-to-do Southern farmer of a century ago. It is a worthy ideal, but can we attain it in this day of a colossal national debt and of billions being spent on defense in the Cold War? Furthermore, are we not already experiencing some of the evil effects of industrialism predicted by the Southern Agrarians in 1930 when they published that memorable symposium, *I'll Take My Stand*?

The status of the slaveholding planter carried its obligations, its ideal of *noblesse oblige.* He must look after his slaves when they were old or sick and unprofitable. He must not permit them to be exploited by overseers or itinerant traders. Except for the field hands on the larger plantations, the slaves were in a sense now difficult to explain, members of the family. The fiery Major Lightfoot in Ellen Glasgow's *The Battle-Ground* finds a low-class white man beating a slave on the public highway. He buys the Negro on the spot and then speaks his mind: "There's no man alive that shall question the divine right of slavery in my presence; but —it is an institution for gentlemen, and you, sir, are a damned scoundrel!"

One of the finest of Virginia gentlemen was Thomas Dabney, who rather than sell his slaves sold his land in Virginia and made the long journey to Mississippi to start life anew. After the Civil War he lost everything he had because in the traditional Virginia fashion he had endorsed notes for a neighbor—in this instance a dishonest man. Once when he was sick and did not know whether he would recover, Dabney said to his children: "I shall have nothing to leave you but a fair name. . . . I shall, if I live, pay every dollar that I owe. If I die, I leave these debts to you to discharge. Do not let my name be dishonored." Fortunately, he lived to pay off his debts. General Sherman, whose one visit to Middle Georgia is well remembered, was reported to have said that he would like to bring every Southern woman to the wash-tub. "He shall never bring my daughters to the wash-tub," said Dabney. He was then in his seventieth year, and for two years he did the family washing himself. In December, 1889, William E. Gladstone in reviewing for the *Nineteenth Century* the life of Thomas Dabney written by his daughter, concluded: "Let no man say, with this book before him, that the age of chivalry has gone, or that Thomas Dabney was not worthy to sit with Sir Percival at the 'table round' of King Arthur."

The first notable treatment of Southerners in American fiction is found in *The Spy* (1821), by James Fenimore Cooper, a New York country gentleman who had close friends among Southerners. Although the locale of the novel is in Westchester County, New York, fully half the leading characters are Southern. The Singletons are from Georgia. Miss Peyton, Dr. Sitgreaves, Captain Jack Lawton and his troopers are Virginians, and so is Major Peyton Dunwoodie, who commands the Virginia horsemen. General Washington also figures in the story, but there is no emphasis upon his Virginian traits. The Virginia troopers are pictured as dashing horsemen, "full of mettle" and inclined to recklessness. "Their manners and conversation" are "a strange mixture of the bluntness of the partisan with the manners of gentlemen." Captain Jack Lawton, who never forgets that he is "a Virginian and a gentleman," is a splendid horseman, a gallant soldier, and the idol of his men. Like a true Virginian, he fights a duel to avenge a wrong done to a woman. He is a generous friend and an implacable enemy. His death at the head of his men, like his life, brings to mind the deaths, in a later war, of "Jeb" Stuart and Turner Ashby, whose last words were "Charge, Virginians, charge!" There is no more lifelike portrait of the Virginia cavalier in fiction; but Captain Lawton is not the idealized soldier of romance. His appearance is somewhat wild; and among his enemies, who call him "the mad Virginian," he has a reputation for ferocity. Many another Virginia gentleman would have agreed with Jack Lawton that "with a full stomach, a stout heart, and a clear conscience . . . a man might bid defiance to the world and its vicissitudes."

It was not long before Southern novelists were following in Cooper's footsteps. There are some notable portraits of Virginia gentlemen in George Tucker's *The Valley of Shenandoah* (1824) and in John Pendleton Kennedy's *Swallow Barn* (1832). These books were quickly followed by Simms's Revolutionary Romances, which include portraits of several South Carolina gentlemen, notably General Francis Marion and the fictitious Captain Porgy, who is perhaps Simms's finest character. The gentry of Charleston and the Low-Country plantations are well described in Simms's *The Golden Christmas* (1852).

Too often in our fiction the gentleman and the lady receive only such conventional treatment as Scott gave to Ivanhoe and Rowena and Cooper to Peyton Dunwoodie and Frances Wharton. There are nevertheless some excellent portraits of Virginia gentlemen found in fiction and written by men who knew intimately the kind of men they wrote about. For Kennedy, whose *Swallow Barn* is our best account in fiction of Virginia plantation life, the chief traits of the Virginia planter gentry were: "The mellow, bland, and sunny luxuriance of her old-time society—its good fellowship, its hearty and constitutional *companionableness,* the thriftless gayety of the people, their dogged but amiable invincibility of opinion, and that overflowing hospitality which knew no ebb. . . ." Kennedy's mother was a Virginian, and he often visited in the Old Dominion. In the Civil War, however, his sympathies were with the Union cause. In March, 1863, he wrote in his journal this less favorable estimate of Virginian traits:

Virginia with its medieval civilization—so slow in progress—so blind to its fate; so steadfast in prejudice, so complacent in its self-esteem. . . . Where are there gentlemen so true, so sweet, so courteous and full of all winning kindness—gentle and brave—as there! Where more lovely women—But where are there men so stubborn in opinion, so crotchety, so flippant and presuming!

For Virginia life in the years immediately following the War between the States there is no better account than that given in *Sketches from Old Virginia* (1897), written by Arthur Granville Bradley, an English gentleman who spent several years in Virginia as a farmer. For Bradley the chief charm of Virginia life was its homespun simplicity.

Now the Doctor was a Southerner of the old school. Nor was he merely a North Carolinian, a Tennesseean, a Kentuckian, or a Georgian—not any, thank you! No; our friend was a Virginian—a real "old-fashioned, blue-blooded, whole-souled, open-handed Virginian." . . . No day passed but the Doctor, in his simple fashion, unconsciously thanked God that he was a Virginian. For did not virtue, valour, honour, gallantry select the Old Dominion in the days of the Stuarts as their special depot, whence, in modified streams, these qualities might be diffused over the less fortunate portions of the Western world?

Although the Doctor was "just and unassuming, kindly and homely,"

He hated Yankees; he hated your new-fangled houses; he hated railroads; he hated breech-loading guns; sights and sounds and things that he was not familiar with at five-and-twenty, he would have none of them when he was between sixty and seventy.

Some memorable descriptions of Virginia gentlemen are to be found in the novels of George Cary Eggleston and in his biography of his older brother Edward, who wrote *The Hoosier Schoolmaster.* The Egglestons were natives of Indiana, but their father was a Virginian, and as young men they visited their relatives in Virginia. In his life of his brother, *The First of the Hoosiers* (1903), George Cary Eggleston gives us a notable portrait of his uncle by marriage, Chastain Cocke, as fine a gentleman as Thomas Dabney. George Cary liked Virginia so much that he fought in the Confederate army. In November, 1875, he published in the *Atlantic Monthly* one of the most charming accounts of Virginia planter life ever written, "The Old Régime in the Old Dominion."

Edward Eggleston, whose sympathies were with the Union cause, included in *The Graysons* (1887) a portrait of the judge who presided over a trial in which the youthful Abraham Lincoln cleared a friend of the charge of murder by producing an almanac to prove that the key witness for the prosecution was lying when he said he saw the murder committed on a brilliant moonlight night:

> [Judge Watkins] was full of the honorable if somewhat irascible pride of a Virginian with a superstitious reverence for his "family." Judge Watkins came of an ancestry famous only for courageously holding up their heads and doing nothing that they considered unworthy of gentlemen. Their greatest pride was that they had always been proud. The judge's coat hung loosely on his frame, and his trousers were generally drawn up in wrinkles so as to show half of his bootlegs. His garments were, moreover, well worn and rather coarse; like his planter ancestors, he never fancied that dress could add anything to the dignity of a gentleman. The substantial distinction of a gentleman, in his estimation, consisted in being of a "good family," and in preferring to lose one's life rather than to lie, and to take another man's life

rather than to suffer the reproach of falsehood or cowardice. It was characteristic of a Virginian of this type to have something like a detestation for clothes, except in so far as they served for decency and warmth; all the great difference which separated a respected gentleman from a despised fop lay in this fierce contempt for appearances. Judge Watkins left fine coats and gold watches for those who needed such decorations; he clothed himself in homespun and family pride.

When I was living in Texas, I sometimes thought that distance from the Old Dominion added to the length and the splendor of the migrating Virginian's pedigree. It seemed to me also that life in the West often served rather to intensify than to modify one's Virginian traits. As Joseph Glover Baldwin put it in *The Flush Times of Alabama and Mississippi,*

> It makes no odds where he goes, he carries Virginia with him. . . . *"Coelum non animum mutant qui trans mare currunt,"* was made for a Virginian. He never gets acclimated elsewhere; he never loses citizenship to the old Home. . . . He may breathe in Alabama, but he lives in Virginia.

In *Pudd'nhead Wilson,* Mark Twain, whose father was a Virginian, described the Howards and the Driscolls in language that might almost have served to characterize his own father:

> In Missouri a recognized superiority attached to any person who hailed from Old Virginia; and this superiority was exalted to eminence when a person of such nativity could also prove descent from the First Families of that great commonwealth. The Howards and Driscolls were of this aristocracy. In their eyes it was a nobility. It had its unwritten laws, and they were as clearly defined and as strict as any that could be found among the printed statutes of the land. The F. F. V. was born a gentleman; his highest duty in life was to watch over that great inheritance and keep it unsmirched.

He must keep his honor spotless. Those laws were his chart; his course was marked out on it; if he swerved from it by so much as half a point of the compass it meant shipwreck to his honor; that is to say, degradation from his rank as a gentleman.

My next example is also from Mark Twain—this time a Kentucky gentleman from *Huckleberry Finn.* Kentucky was of course originally a part of Virginia. Colonel Grangerford is the head of one of the two families who keep up the traditional feud and shoot at one another on sight.

Col. Grangerford was a gentleman, you see. He was a gentleman all over; and so was his family. He was well born, as the saying is, and that's worth as much in a man as it is in a horse, so the Widow Douglas said, and nobody ever denied that she was of the first aristocracy in our town; and pap he always said it, too, though he warn't no more quality than a mudcat himself. Col. Grangerford was very tall and very slim, and had a darkish-paly complexion, not a sign of red in it anywheres; he was clean-shaved every morning all over his thin face, and he had the thinnest kind of lips, and the thinnest kind of nostrils, and a high nose, and heavy eyebrows, and the blackest kind of eyes, sunk so deep back that they seemed like they was looking out of caverns at you, as you may say. His forehead was high, and his hair was gray and straight and hung to his shoulders. His hands was long and thin, and every day of his life he put on a clean shirt and a full suit from head to foot made out of linen so white it hurt your eyes to look at it; and on Sundays he wore a blue tailcoat with brass buttons on it. He carried a mahogany cane with a silver head to it. There warn't no frivolishness about him, not a bit, and he warn't ever loud. He was as kind as he could be—you could feel that, you know, and so you had confidence. Sometimes he smiled, and it was good to see; but when he straightened himself up like a liberty-pole, and the lightning begun to flicker out from under his eyebrows, you wanted to climb a tree first, and find out what the matter was afterwards.

John William De Forest, a Connecticut Yankee who had been in the South for many months before, during, and after the Civil War, saw a striking resemblance between the traits of the Southern gentleman and those of the professional soldier: "Notably brave, punctilious as to honor, pugnacious to quarrelsomeness, authoritative to imperiousness, generous to extravagance, somewhat formal in his courtesy, somewhat grandiose in his self-respect, there is hardly an agreeable or disagreeable trait in him which you cannot find in the officers of most armies." The "central trait of the 'chivalrous Southron' " was in De Forest's estimation "an intense respect for virility."

> If you will fight, if you are strong and skilful enough to kill your antagonist, if you can govern or influence the common herd, if you can ride a dangerous horse over rough country, if you are a good shot or an expert swordsman, if you stand by your own opinions unflinchingly, if you do your level best on whisky, if you are a devil of a fellow with women, if, in short, you show vigorous masculine attributes, he will grant you his respect.

The remarkable courage of the Confederate soldier De Forest cynically accounted for by saying: "The bullet-hole was a mere question of time, and why not open one's arms to it on the field of glory?" There were no doubt Southern gentlemen of that kind, but the great leaders of the Confederate armies—Lee, Stuart, Wade Hampton, John B. Gordon, and the Johnstons, Albert Sidney and Joseph Eggleston—were not of the dueling, swaggering variety.

As I said in my last lecture, the number of planters as opposed to yeomen farmers was quite small when compared with the numbers in our Southern legend of the Old South. In Virginia in 1860 in a population of over one million whites there were only 52,128 men who owned any slaves. There were only 114 who owned as many as one hundred. At least nineteen out of every twenty slaveholders was a yeoman, who held two or three slaves and worked in the tobacco fields beside them. The great planters were few in numbers, but it was from their class that as a rule the people chose their representatives in Congress and the General Assembly. The economic interpretation of history would suggest the doubtful conclusion that their status as property holders led them to neglect the classes who were less fortunate. Be that as it may, the ante-bellum Southern politicians were as free from graft and corruption as any this country has had elsewhere. Arthur Lee, after a lifetime of service to Virginia and the other colonies, wrote: "The science of government is no trifling matter. It requires education and experience, it requires the habit of great worlds and great men, it requires the leisure which independent fortune gives and the elevation of mind which birth and rank impart. Without these you might as well attempt to make Sèvres china out of common earth as statesmen and politicians out of men bred and born in the sordid occurrences of common life." That is so remote from the professed attitude of both political parties nowadays as to be shocking; and yet one may well wonder why it is that since the Civil War Virginia has given us so few statesmen comparable to those who grew up in a slaveholding society.

The Virginia lady was thoroughly feminine. Her virtues and her ideals were not those of her great-grandchildren. She was often well-read, but she did not wish to be regarded as intellectual. In Ellen Glasgow's *The Battle-Ground* Mrs. Ambler remarks to her daughter

Betty: "Women do not need as much sense as men, my dear. If the Lord had wanted you to be clever, He would have made you a man." By modern standards the Virginia lady's life was provincial and narrow, but she was highly honored, especially if she was beautiful and charming.

In Virginia the belle was an institution. With a touch of exaggeration Mrs. Burton Harrison wrote: "In those days a Southern beauty tripped through life on a path strewn with roses, hearts, and darts. All men became Sir Calidores on her behalf." Virginia still produces beautiful women, but the Southern belle is no longer an institution. If you are interested in her present status, you should read in *Holiday* for November, 1959, Frances Gray Patton's "Anatomy of the Southern Belle."

The Virginia matron is pictured in fiction as delicate, frail, and overworked. The planter might delegate some of his responsibilities to an overseer if he was wealthy enough to employ one, but the matron was not always fortunate enough to have a spinster aunt, sister, or cousin to assist in the discharge of her numerous duties. In addition to the training of her children, the direction of the household, and the entertainment of numerous guests, she had the care of the black family on her hands. She had to superintend the making of clothing, the distribution of provisions, and the cultivation of the flower and vegetable gardens. She looked after the servants when ill, watched over their conduct, and gave them religious instruction. Besides all this, "Ole Miss" often sewed, cooked, and washed her fine china dishes with her own hands. She was the keystone of the whole domestic establishment, and her big basket of keys was the symbol of her authority.

Sometimes, like Madam Esmond-Warrington in Thackeray's *The Virginians,* she became a little tyrant. One Virginia matron, when asked how many slaves her husband owned, replied: "Sir, my husband owns a thousand negroes, and only one slave; and that is myself."

I regret that time does not suffice for me to discuss the Virginia lady as fully as she deserves. You may be sure that the Virginia lady of plantation days was not in any way unworthy of her father, her husband, or her sons. Indeed, she had a larger part than any other human being in the development of the Virginia gentlemen in her family. Those who wish to know more of her will find many fine portraits of Virginia women in the novels of Ellen Glasgow. Her women characters seem to me much more lifelike than the idealized heroines of Thomas Nelson Page and James Lane Allen.

The Virginia novelists have given us many fine portraits of the planter families. They have on the whole neglected the other and more numerous classes, in part perhaps because the writers themselves belonged to Virginia's First Families. Certainly they have often given to their heroes and heroines the equivalent of their own pedigrees. Thomas Nelson Page opened his novel, *Gordon Keith,* with this statement: "Gordon Keith was the son of a gentleman," and until the reader came to the last page, the novelist rarely allowed him to forget that Gordon Keith's father was a Virginia gentleman.

In *The Old South* (1892) Page himself has traced to its source the most striking incident in his best-known short story, "Marse Chan":

Some years ago I was shown a worn and faded letter written on old Confederate paper with pale Confederate ink. It had been taken from the breast-pocket of a dead private of a Georgia regiment after one of the battles around Richmond. It was from his sweetheart. They were plain and illiterate people, for it was badly written and badly spelled. In it she told him that she loved him; that she had always loved him since they had gone to school together, in the little log schoolhouse in the woods; that she was sorry she had always treated him so badly, and that now, if he would get a furlough and come home, she would marry him.

Then, as if fearful that this temptation might prove too strong to be resisted, there was a little postscript scrawled across the blue Confederate paper: "Don't come without a furlough, for if you don't come honorable, I won't marry you."

Some years after writing "Marse Chan" Page used the same situation in "Little Darby," the story of a Virginia poor-white who like Marse Chan gets his furlough, so to speak, through death on the battlefield. Page, as he wrote to Arthur Hobson Quinn, had finally come to feel that "it was due to that class that I should testify with whatever power I might possess, to their devotion to the South." He did not, however, in either story make his hero a Georgian.

You have probably heard the apocryphal story of what a Virginia lady said to a North Carolinian who had asked her: "What became of the Second Families of Virginia?" "Why," she responded, "who else do you suppose populated North Carolina?" The earlier Virginia novelists had not much to say about the poor-whites and the various members of the middle classes. Ellen Glasgow, however, made much of the rise of the yeomen and the poor-whites in the years following the Civil War. In *Barren Ground* (1925) she explained the wide difference in meaning in Virginia between the phrases "good people" and "good family":

> . . . "good people," a comprehensive term . . . implies, to discriminating Virginians, the exact opposite of the phrase "a good family." The good families of the state have preserved, among other things, custom, history, tradition, romantic fiction, and the Episcopal Church. The good people, according to the records of clergymen, which are the only surviving records, have preserved nothing except themselves. Ignored alike by history and fiction, they have their inconspicuous place in the social strata midway between the lower gentility and the upper class of "poor white," a position which encourages the useful rather than the ornamental public virtues.

Did you ever notice that in fiction, whether realistic or romantic, it is as a rule either the gentry or the peasantry or their modern equivalents that play the leading roles? This is as true of Scott and Tolstoy as it is of John Esten Cooke and Thomas Nelson Page. The upper middle class, which buys more novels than any other, does not care to see itself depicted in fiction unless it can see in the hero a man of its own class rising in the social scale. The great middle class was shocked to discover that it was being satirized in Sinclair Lewis's *Babbitt* and *Main Street.*

There are some notable gentlemen in the novels of Ellen Glasgow, who herself belonged to one of Richmond's first families. There was, however, no glamour for her in the status of gentleman or lady. She was, as she later realized, "a born rebel." For the leading character of her first novel, *The Descendant* (1897), she chose a poor-white who was also an illegitimate child. Her female relatives advised her: "If you must write, do write of ladies and gentlemen." One of her elderly kinsmen who had looked into *The Descendant,* exclaimed: "But it is incredible that a well-brought-up Southern girl should even know what a bastard is!" The leading character in the novel defines the word "aristocrat" as "one who sits down to think about what his grandfather has done while other men are doing something themselves." Ellen Glasgow lived long enough to witness the sorry role played by the Southern gentleman in novels by younger Southern writers. In 1935 she confided to a friend: "I am unable to accept the comfortable theory that all the cruelty in this section is confined within the feeble bosoms of degenerate aristocrats. For one thing, there are not enough aristocrats left among us to make one first-class sadist. The few that are left seldom open a book, and too many of these Southern horrors have a literary, not to say a theatrical, odor."

Of Ellen Glasgow's many fine portraits of Virginia gentlemen I shall single out two. One of the most admirable is General David Archbald of *The Sheltered Life* (1932), "a lover of wisdom, a humane and civilized soul, oppressed by the burden of tragic remembrance." ". . . into his lonely spirit," says the author, "I have put much of my ultimate feeling about life. He represents the tragedy, wherever it appears, of the civilized man in a world that is not civilized." At the other extreme is Judge Gamaliel Bland Honeywell of *The Romantic Comedians* (1926) to whom she refers in *A Certain Measure* as "a collective portrait of several Virginians of an older school, who are still unafraid to call themselves gentlemen." There is a family resemblance between the philandering Judge Honeywell and the Richmond lawyer whom she calls "Harold" and to whom she was once engaged. After his flirtation with Queen Marie of Roumania she dipped her pen in acid and drew his portrait in *The Woman Within.*

In real life as in fiction there are Southern types that

are far from admirable; and, if we except the actual criminal, perhaps the professional Southerner is the most detestable. Here is O. Henry's description of "Major (by misplaced courtesy) Wentworth Caswell" in "A Municipal Report," which has its locale in Nashville, Tennessee:

> Major Caswell banged the bar with his fist, and the first gun at Fort Sumter re-echoed. When he fired the last one at Appomattox I began to hope. But then he began on family trees, and demonstrated that Adam was only a third cousin of a collateral branch of the Caswell family. Genealogy disposed of, he took up, to my distaste, his private family matters. He spoke of his wife, traced her descent back to Eve, and profanely denied any possible rumor that she may have had relations in the land of Nod.

"Major" Caswell, you may remember, has no income except what he steals from his wife's earnings as a writer and from what old Uncle Caesar manages to earn for his former mistress by driving an ancient and decrepit carriage. We feel no regret when we learn that Uncle Caesar has killed the contemptible "Major."

That is the worst type of "Southern gentleman." F. Hopkinson Smith's *Colonel Carter of Cartersville* (1891) takes to New York City a Virginia gentleman who is excessively chivalrous and sentimental but also "frank, generous, tender-hearted . . . proud of his ancestry, proud of his State, and proud of himself; believing in states' rights, slavery, and the Confederacy. . . ." Colonel Carter seems almost a caricature of the genuine ante-bellum Virginia gentleman, out of place in a great Northern city.

Colonel Carter is not unlike Mark Twain's Colonel Sellers, who figures in *The Gilded Age* (1873) as the penniless dreamer of money to be made by the million in fantastic ways. Once on the witness stand in a murder trial Colonel Sellers was asked: "What is your occupation?" His answer was: "A gentleman, sir." That answer no doubt brought a laugh from many of Mark Twain's readers; and yet a prominent New England gentleman, James Russell Lowell, could maintain that being a gentleman is "a profession of greater consequence than is generally conceived." The value to American society of the country gentleman is nowhere better expounded than in James Fenimore Cooper's *The American Democrat* (1838), written at the very time when the Jacksonian Democrats were glorifying the common man at the expense of Cooper's own class. Yet years later in the South, where the gentlemanly ideal lingered longest, a Virginia poet, Daniel Bedinger Lucas, could boast: "I am a Democrat; I am a Virginian; I am a gentleman." In the old days what more indeed could a young man ask? Well, perhaps a little more. Do you remember the expressive epigram (which I do not quote for its literary value)?

> All I want in this creation
> Is a pretty little wife and a big plantation.

The old plantations are gone. After the emancipation of the slaves most of them were broken up and sold for debt and fell into the hands of small farmers, white and black. Hardly one is now in the hands of the descendants of the original owners, and those who now own them must draw on incomes derived from other sources than farming to keep them up. With the increasing industrialization of the South the old way of life and the old ideals began rapidly to fade. The drift was from country to town and from town to city, often a Northern or Western city. The economic basis of the country gentleman's way of life disappeared, as it had earlier disappeared in the North. I like De Forest's story of a young Kentuckian of good Virginia family who after living for a time in New York City, said:

> "I can't stand this any longer. I can't respect myself when I am run against a dozen times a day by Irishmen, Jews, Yankees, and all kinds of busy people. I am of no consequence here; nobody cares whether I am a gentleman or not—whether I am angry or pleased; nobody values me as I know I ought to be valued. I must go South again—go where there is more elbow-room—go where I can make myself known. I detest a city where seven hundred thousand people tread on my toes, and haven't a moment's leisure to apologize, and don't even know that my name is Peyton."

Even in the smaller Southern cities, like Macon and Durham—not to mention Richmond and Atlanta—it is difficult for the urban Southerner of our time to emulate the virtues or the way of life of the gentleman planter and his lady of the old regime. Except in the most casual fashion they rarely know their urban or suburban neighbors. Hospitality of the traditional sort costs too much in cold cash as the housewife cannot fail to realize every time she visits a supermarket. The Negro servants, if she has any, are a strange people, not in any sense members of the family.

Of course the urban Southerner admires George Washington, General Lee, and Sidney Lanier; but they lived in another world altogether. Ours is the atomic age, the space age, the age of electronics. We live in the shadow of an enormous national debt, and everything that happened before 1914 is ancient history. The middle-aged Southerner discovers that the science he studied in high school or college is obsolete and has been replaced by something which appears mysterious and a little terrifying when his teen-age daughter in blue jeans with a test-tube in her hands tries to explain it to him. The old Virginia gentleman would have agreed with a distinguished New England gentleman who wrote in his journal for 1833: "God defend me from ever looking at a man as an animal." That was Ralph Waldo Emerson. Darwin thought otherwise, and so did Sigmund Freud. Women as well as men are animals, and they can no longer expect to be put up on pedestals and worshiped. The radical change in our sex mores is vividly depicted in Ellen Glasgow's *They Stooped to Folly* (1929), which tells us what happened to the women of three successive generations who lost their virtue. De Forest thought that the honor system practiced in Southern universities and colleges was the finest manifestation of the Southern gentleman's code. But how many Southern institutions of learning today have an honor system or one that really functions?

If we may believe Stuart Chase and other critics of our way of life, there has been a notable decline in the American's sense of integrity. Perhaps Thomas Jefferson was right when he wrote that farmers "are the most vigorous, the most independant [*sic*], the most virtuous, & they are tied to their country & wedded to it's [*sic*] liberty & interests by the most lasting bonds." Nowadays we are not independent farmers. We are employees, and all of us—even in college faculties—have our superiors whom we had better please if we are to expect advancement in rank and an increase in salary. The Virginia gentleman was nobody's "yes-man."

Every student of history or literature must have wished that the age in which his lot is irrevocably cast were in some respects more like the age of Pericles, or Augustus, or Elizabeth I. But one must not allow oneself to become a mere *laudator temporis acti*; nor, on the other hand, must one close his eyes to the short-comings of the present age. Bertrand Russell was not far wrong when he wrote in an essay entitled "On Being Modern-Minded": "Our age is the most parochial since Homer. . . . We imagine ourselves at the apex of intelligence, and cannot believe that the quaint clothes and cumbrous phrases of former times can have invested people and thoughts that are still worthy of our attention."

The Emersonian doctrine of Compensation is hardly recognized as a scientific law in any textbook on physics or chemistry; but, if taken empirically, it has its value for the modern-minded. "Society," wrote Emerson, "never advances. . . . For everything that is given something is taken." Modern methods of transportation have brought about a decline in manners if not in morals, or so it seems. The industrialization of the South is raising the income of the average family in this area to a higher level than prevailed anywhere in this country a century ago. We cannot any longer accept Senator Hammond's premise that there must always be a "mudsill" class to perform the necessary drudgery. Those unpleasant tasks, we hope, will in this day of gadgets and automation soon be performed by machines. That is a consummation devoutly to be wished if we can learn to spend wisely the leisure given us by a four- or five-day work week. On the other hand, the industrialization of the South has brought us new problems; and it is sad to note how little we in the South have learned from the experience of either old or New England, both of which entered the industrial era earlier than the Southern states. Furthermore, since the Second World War our country has taken upon itself international responsibilities for which I am not sure that our political leaders in either party have the wisdom or the skill needed to carry out.

There are powerful forces—economic, social, and political—which tend to wipe out all differences between the South and the North, the East and the West, and to reduce American life to a single monotonous pattern. Now beyond question there are elements in our Southern tradition which we should be glad to see disappear; but my hope is that we can preserve some of the best "values of Southern culture, history, and literature." If these values are to be preserved, we must look primarily to educated men and women to keep them alive, for few others have a sense of history or appreciate fully the value of our inherited ideals. Our young people need to be taught to look to other models than playboys, professional athletes, millionaires, and show people. They need to become better acquainted with the best Southern men and women of the past. For Ellen Glasgow, Virginia's past was "like a hall hung with rare and wonderful tapestries, or perhaps it would be truer to say that it is like a cathedral illumined by the gold and wine-colour of stained glass windows." For me Virginia's past is more like the National Portrait Gallery in London, which on a brief visit a few years ago gave me a keener sense of the men and women who have made England great than all the monuments in that great city. For Virginia I like to imagine a gallery containing the portraits of such men as Washington, Jefferson, Lee, Thomas Dabney, and Woodrow Wilson. For me it also includes some of the notable gentlemen depicted in Virginia fiction, every one of whom must have had somewhere at least one original in real life: Page's Dr. Cary in *Red Rock,* Kennedy's Frank Meriwether in *Swallow Barn,* and Ellen Glasgow's General Archbald of *The Sheltered Life,* a "civilized man in a world that is not civilized." It was these men and men like them who have passed on to us our highest political and social ideals, and they still stand as models of excellence in all the manly qualities which the Elizabethans summed up in the word "Magnanimity."

LECTURE THREE

Georgia in Literature

WHEN I BEGAN TEACHING, THERE WERE FEW COURSES IN American literature offered in any American college or university, and for some years most of my classes were in English literature or composition. Since my primary interest was in America, I noted with special interest any allusions to this country which I found in the writings of English authors. In 1936 I included some of these in my *American Life in Literature*. I carefully labeled all these selections as English, and yet on final examinations I was repeatedly informed by careless students that Charles Dickens was a great American novelist and that Matthew Arnold, though a very dull writer, was considered a fine American critic. In the next edition of my anthology I placed all the selections from the English writers in an appendix.

The English writers have taken widely divergent attitudes toward America. For the Elizabethan dramatists it was the last refuge of the destitute and the dishonest. For Daniel Defoe Virginia was a place where the convict could become an honest man and rehabilitate himself. Other English writers shared the attitude of Samuel Johnson, who once denounced the Americans as "a race of convicts [who] ought to be thankful for any thing we allow them short of hanging." In my last lecture I noted the very different view expressed in Michael Drayton's "Ode to the Virginian Voyage." A century and more later Bishop Berkeley wrote: "Westward the course of empire takes its way." In America he foresaw "another golden age, / The rise of empire and of arts."

In "The Deserted Village" Oliver Goldsmith pictured the unhappy fate of the English villagers who left their homes and migrated to a land which I take to be Georgia. In Goldsmith's "wild Altama" you will perhaps recognize the Altamaha River.

> Ah, no. To distant climes, a dreary scene,
> Where half the convex world intrudes between,
> Through torrid tracts with fainting steps they go,
> Where wild Altama murmurs to their woe.
> Far different there from all that charm'd before,
> The various terrors of that horrid shore;
> Those blazing suns that dart a downward ray,
> And fiercely shed intolerable day;
> Those matted woods where birds forget to sing,
> But silent bats in drowsy clusters cling;
> Those pois'nous fields with rank luxuriance crown'd,
> Where the dark scorpion gathers death around;
> Where at each step the stranger fears to wake
> The rattling terrors of the vengeful snake;
> Where crouching tigers wait their hapless prey,
> And savage men more murd'rous still than they;
> While oft in whirls the mad tornado flies,
> Mingling the ravag'd landscape with the skies.
> Far different these from every former scene,
> The cooling brook, the grassy-vested green,
> The breezy covert of the warbling grove,
> That only shelter'd thefts of harmless love.

Two greater English poets, Coleridge and Wordsworth, were fascinated by the vivid descriptions of the flora and fauna of Georgia and Florida which they found in the *Travels* of William Bartram. In *The Road to Xanadu* the late John Livingston Lowes brilliantly demonstrated the use that Coleridge made of Bartram's book in "The Rime of the Ancient Mariner." Wordsworth also used Bartram's *Travels* but in a manner surprising in so fervent a worshiper of nature. His "Ruth" is the story of an English country girl who is wooed and won by a young Englishman who has been in Georgia and is quite fascinating in his Cherokee war bonnet. Not long after their marriage the faithless husband deserts his wife, and the poet makes it clear that it is the Georgia climate and landscape that have brought out what was potentially evil in the lover's character. The influence of Mother Nature, one concludes, is beneficent only in the British Isles.

Evidently if Georgia was to be depicted in literature in a manner to please American readers, the state must look to native Americans if indeed not to native Georgians. Yet the first notable piece of writing to come out of Georgia gave an even more unfavorable view of the colony than anything written by the English poets. This was *A True and Historical Narrative of the Colony of Georgia,* published in Charleston and London in 1741. The title page informs us that the authors were Patrick Tailfer, M.D., Hugh Anderson, M.A., David Douglas, and Others, "Landholders in Georgia, at present in Charleston, South Carolina." These embittered Scots had not prospered in Georgia, and they blamed the government for their misfortunes. They had probably left Georgia to escape arrest and imprisonment. In their little book they speak feelingly of the great hardship in so hot a climate of not being permitted to own slaves and to buy rum. They make one think of Marx and Lenin when they speak of "a new kind of tyranny." They allege that the new clergyman in the colony—his name was John Wesley—had shown that his real aim was, as they phrased it, "to enslave our minds, as a necessary preparative to enslaving our bodies." The mocking Dedication of the book to General Oglethorpe is a notable piece of satirical writing. The authors conclude that "the poor inhabitants of Georgia are scattered over the face of the earth; her plantations a wild; her towns a desert; her villages in rubbish; her improvements a by-word, and her liberties a jest, an object of pity to friends, and of insult, contempt and ridicule to enemies."

Most of what is memorable in the literature of Georgia has come not from the coastal region but from Middle Georgia. In that part of the state there were some large-scale planters, but most of the farmers were yeomen, who if they owned any slaves worked in the fields beside them. To Joel Chandler Harris it was "the most truly democratic region in the world. The class distinctions that we read about in the fiction produced before the war, and in some of the Northern objections advanced against the South, had no existence in Middle Georgia." Many of the early settlers came from Virginia and the Carolinas at the time when Georgia was in, or just emerging from, the frontier stage of society. You would never guess it from his dialect, but doesn't Harris somewhere tell us that Uncle Remus was born in Virginia?

If you have read Sidney Lanier's "The New South," you will remember his brief description of what one can see when one stands at a certain spot and "looks off up and across the Ocmulgee River," or, as he notes, "As one stands in the street of Vineville, a pleasant collection of residences suburban to Macon." Here, he says:

. . . the little valleys everywhere run with living waters, asking grasses and cattle and quiet grist-mills; all manner of timbers for economic uses and trees for finer arts cover the earth; in short, here is such a neighborly congregation of climates, soils, minerals and vegetables, that within a compass of many a hundred-acre farm a man may find wherewithal to build his house of stone, of brick, of oak, or of pine, to furnish it in woods that would delight the most curious eye, and, to supply his family with all the necessaries, most of the comforts, and many of the luxuries, of the whole world. It is the country of homes.

Sidney Lanier and Joel Chandler Harris are the best-known writers that Middle Georgia has given the nation, but there are numerous others that Georgians at least should remember: Francis Orray Ticknor, Thomas Holley Chivers, Richard Malcolm Johnston, Harry Stillwell Edwards, Augusta Jane Evans, Augustus Baldwin Longstreet, William Tappan Thompson, and Charles Henry Smith ("Bill Arp"). Paul Hamilton Hayne was a native of Charleston, but he spent the last twenty years of his life in Middle Georgia.

In December, 1914, Fred Lewis Pattee, then studying the literature of the New South, received an interesting letter from "Holly Bluff, Macon, Ga." The letter was from Harry Stillwell Edwards, who thought that Wesleyan College had much to do with Georgia's literary development:

. . . I wish to state as my personal opinion that Georgia's literary development, which is undoubtedly more extensive than that of other Southern States, is due to the intellectual and spiritual soil or environment produced by this College in the fifty years of its existence previous to 1890. You will understand how this can be true though the mothers of the State's best known writers may not have been graduates. In my youth, every girl associate I had was of this college. Its atmosphere was everywhere apparent. To-day its graduates lead all over the State.

In November, 1874, when he visited Macon, Bret Harte wrote to his wife: "I have heard no better English spoken anywhere—nor as good—as among the wives and daughters of this State of Georgia." Edwards did not mention other institutions of learning in Georgia—Oglethorpe, Mercer, and the State University in Athens—but you may be sure that they, too, had a part in preparing the ground for what the state has contributed to the literature of the New South.

Until the twentieth century, the Virginia novelists generally neglected all classes but the First Families and their faithful servants. The humorists and the novelists of Georgia, however, had a great deal to say about the middle and lower classes, white and black. In this respect they anticipated the Southern novelists of the present century who if they notice the planter gentry generally picture them as degenerate. The Georgia writers knew that the Southern yeoman often was—and is—a very individual person rich in such traits of character as ought to catch the eye of a writer. One of the finest portraits of the Georgia farmer appears in the title essay of Donald Davidson's *Still Rebels, Still Yankees.* The yeoman often had a keen sense of humor. He loved a good story, and often he could tell one with a skill and charm that were relished by his rural auditors.

In the early nineteenth century parts of Georgia were still in the frontier stage of society, but they were changing rapidly. Back in the older states of Virginia and South Carolina every man knew his place. On the frontier, however, people judged a man by his dress, his speech, and his pretensions until they found him to be something different from what he appeared or professed to be. On the frontier there were of course many men of sterling character, but there were also numerous fools and suckers, and naturally there were rascals and sharpers to prey upon them. Joseph Glover Baldwin, who as a young Virginia lawyer migrated to the Old Southwest, wrote in *The Flush Times of Alabama and Mississippi:* "The condition of society may be imagined: – vulgarity – ignorance – fussy and arrogant pretension – unmitigated rowdyism – bullying insolence, if they did not rule the hour *seemed* to wield unchecked dominion." It was a North Carolina newspaperman, Charles Napoleon Bonaparte Evans, who created the character of Jesse Holmes the Fool-Killer, and another North Carolinian, Johnson Jones Hooper, who, while living in Alabama, created that rare sharper, Captain Simon Suggs. This prize rascal, who once robbed the congregation at a camp-meeting, expressed his philosophy when he said: "It is good to be shifty in a New Country." The Old Southwest, extending from Georgia to Texas and including Kentucky, Tennessee, and Arkansas, was an immensely fertile field for the humorist. Here were Southern types which had been left undepicted since the time of William Byrd, who described with some skill and a little malice the shiftless whites whom he found along the North Carolina border. It was high time that American writers gave some attention to these backwoodsmen, crackers, poorwhites, Yankee peddlers, mountaineers, riverboatmen, and thrifty farmers.

The material was rich, but how could a young writer manage to find or devise the right technique for exploiting it? A young Georgia lawyer who had graduated from Yale was the first of the Southern humorists to find the answer to this problem; and the result was that minor classic, *Georgia Scenes,* by Augustus Baldwin Longstreet. Edgar Allan Poe, who reviewed it in the *Southern Literary Messenger* in March, 1836, rightly hailed it as "a sure omen of better days for the literature of the South." *Georgia Scenes* was a very influential book, and Middle Georgia became a favorite background of the humorists who followed Longstreet. In the Duke University Library there is a very long letter from Joel Chandler Harris to Professor William Malone Baskervill, of Vanderbilt University, the first scholar to make a serious study of any aspect of Southern literature. I quote a few sentences.

By-the-by, if you will take a map of Georgia, pick out Putnam county; and then put your finger on the counties surrounding it—Morgan, Greene, Hancock, Baldwin, Jones and Jasper—you will have under your thumb the seat of Southern humor. Major Jones's Courtship belongs to Morgan county. Colonel Richard Malcolm Johnston's characters to Hancock. Unc' Remus was in Putnam. Simon Suggs was a native of Jasper. Polly Peablossom was from Baldwin. Jonce Hooper went to school in Monticello (Jasper), when a boy and there saw Simon Suggs.

Neither the early humorists nor the literary critics realized that books like *Georgia Scenes* had any real literary value. Of course everybody read the humorists' stories and laughed over them, for the newspapers spread them far and wide. Poe of course was an exception; and a Yankee from Vermont, William Trotter Porter, saw the sketches of the humorists as a new type of literature. He published many of their sketches in his sporting magazine, the *Spirit of the Times,* and he gave every encouragement to the Southern humorists to write and to publish. Today the student of our literature sees the Southern humorists as in a sense pioneer realists and local colorists better worth reading than the romantic and sentimental novelists that were favored by many readers. The tradition of Southern humor reached its climax in Mark Twain, whose parents were Southerners and who grew up in a slaveholding town in Missouri. The humorists were also, as I have suggested, forerunners of the local colorists of the New South, some of whom, like Harris and Edwards, had remarkable humorous gifts. In Georgia the line runs from Longstreet and William Tappan Thompson through Richard Malcolm Johnston and Charles Henry Smith to Harris and Edwards. Johnston began writing as a humorist, following the example of Longstreet and Thompson; he ended as a writer of Middle Georgia local-color stories which he was able to market in Northern literary magazines.

The humorists were for the most part educated young men, lawyers, doctors, soldiers, journalists, who had an eye for character, enjoyed a good story, and liked to tell one. Most of them had read Addison, Goldsmith, Scott, and Irving; but they owed much less to these writers than our early historical romancers owed to Scott. The strongest influence, I think, was the oral one. In the old days one could hear many good stories told on Saturday afternoons at country stores, in county towns on court days, on steamboat or stage coach or railway, at the dinner table in many a home. Southerners loved good talk better than reading and writing, and they still do. Somehow the humorists managed to capture the flavor and the accent of Southern speech and record it with some skill on the printed page.

Students of literary history are familiar with the alternating periods in which literary conventions are built up and then, when they have lost their usefulness, are discarded by young rebels who loudly proclaim a return to nature. Wordsworth, rejecting the artificial poetic diction of his predecessors, advocated the employment of "the language of real life," and a little over a century later the Imagist poets turned to "the language of common speech." Among our twentieth-century poets Robert Frost has caught as no one else has caught the full flavor of the New England dialect; and Ernest Hemingway has perhaps better than others recorded what with some exaggeration H. L. Mencken called the "American language." Hemingway and Faulkner have both said that *Huckleberry Finn* is our first *American* classic. That book is written in Huck's own variety of Southern speech. Like Harris and their humorist predecessors, Mark Twain found it easier to write like an American when he wrote in dialect. So also did Harris and Harte and many another American writer of fiction, for our dialects are only slight variations from our ubiquitous American colloquial English.

Hawthorne and Poe are major figures in our literature, but the literary language they wrote is English rather than American, or so it seems to readers of today. In Hawthorne's *The Blithedale Romance* (1852) this brief dialogue takes place between the narrator, Miles Coverdale, and Hollingsworth, the moving spirit in the Blithedale community, which he now plans to abandon.

"Is Zenobia to take part in your enterprise?" I asked.

"She is," said Hollingsworth.

"She! the beautiful!—the gorgeous!" I exclaimed. "And how have you prevailed with such a woman to work in this squalid element?"

"Through no base methods, as you seem to suspect," he answered, "but by addressing whatever is best and noblest in her."

I cannot believe that even educated New Englanders talked quite like that in the mid-nineteenth century.

Hawthorne's characters speak in his own highly polished prose style, which is excellent; but most readers today are not willing to accept the convention which dictated his practice. For us dialogue must have the accent and the flavor of actual talk.

Now let me read you a bit of dialogue from one of Longstreet's best stories, "The Fight," written twenty years earlier than Hawthorne's romance. In this story we are introduced to Longstreet's best character, Ransy Sniffle, a victim of what we now know as the hookworm disease. Ransy Sniffle never seems to be really alive except when he is "witnessing, fomenting, or talking about a fight." He has long tried to bring about a fight between Billy Stallings and Bob Durham, each the champion in his own part of the county; but the two men happen to be friends and see no reason why they should fight. Ransy finds his long-sought opportunity to provoke a fight as he listens to a conversation in Zeph Atwater's store. Mrs. Durham and Mrs. Stallings, who do not know one another, are both in a hurry, and each insists on being waited upon first.

"Have you any Turkey-red?" said Mrs. S.

"Have you any curtain calico?" said Mrs. D. at the same moment.

"Yes, ladies," said Mr. Atwater, "I have both."

"Then help me first," said Mrs. D., "for I'm in a hurry."

"I'm in as great a hurry as she is," said Mrs. S., "and I'll thank you to help me first."

"And, pray, who are you, madam?" continued the other.

"Your betters, madam," was the reply.

At this moment Billy Stallings stepped in. "Come," said he, "Nancy, let's be going; it's getting late."

"I'd a been gone half an hour ago," she replied, "if it hadn't been for that impudent huzzy."

"Who do you call an impudent huzzy, you nasty, good-for-nothing, snaggle-toothed gaub of fat, you?" returned Mrs. D.

"Look here, woman," said Billy, "have you got a husband here? If you have, I'll *lick* him till he learns to teach you better manners, you *sassy* heifer you."

At this moment something was seen to rush out of the store as if ten thousand hornets were stinging it; crying, "Take care —let me go—don't hold me—where's Bob Durham?" It was Ransy Sniffle, who had been listening in breathless delight to all that had passed.

"Yonder's Bob, setting on the Courthouse steps," cried one. "What's the matter?"

"Don't talk to me!" said Ransy. "Bob Durham, you'd better go long yonder, and take care of your wife. They're playing hell with her there, in Zeph Atwater's store. Dod etarnally darn my soul, if any man was to talk to my wife as Bill Stallions is talking to yours, if I wouldn't drive blue blazes through him in less than no time."

Billy Stallings is naturally disconcerted to find that he has been bawling out his friend's wife; but he says: "Well, it an't worth while to go over it; I've said enough for a fight: and if you'll step out, we'll settle it!"

Longstreet was an accomplished mimic and a good story-teller. He also had a fine ear for the niceties of the "American language" as it was spoken in the Georgia backwoods over a century ago. And according to George Philip Krapp, whose *The English Language in America* is still standard, it was on the Southern frontier that we first find clearly marked the characteristics of American speech. The writing of dialect stories is now out of fashion, but it was through the careful study and recording of Southern, Western, and New England dialects—all of which have a strong family likeness—that our novelists learned to write like Americans.

Before we discuss the literature of the New South, in which Georgia played a leading part, let us look at Middle Georgia as it appeared in November, 1874, to one of the most popular short-story writers of the period.

From Milledgeville on November 4 Bret Harte wrote to his wife: "I have had occasion to change my views of the South very materially, and from what I have seen am quite satisfied that the North is profoundly ignorant of the real sentiments and condition of the people." Three days later he wrote from Macon that he felt as though he were "travelling in a foreign land, and among a foreign people." He was pained by the spectacle of "the utter devastation and ruin brought by the war—and struck *always* with the noble resignation of those that have suffered." Harte was of course radically mistaken in concluding that he was standing "by the bedside of a ruined and slowly dying people," for the New South was shortly to emerge like the fabled phoenix from the ashes left in the wake of invading armies. He found the Georgians "uniformly kind and courteous" and "old-fashioned in everything—in literature, in art, in dress"; yet, as I have already noted, he wrote that nowhere had he "heard better English spoken . . . nor as good—as among the wives and daughters of this State of Georgia."

Harte was trying to write a novel about California, but in Georgia California seemed remote. He could not write; he could only "absorb." "How could I," he wrote, "expect to interest a people who were infinitely quainter and more original, more pathetic, more ludicrous than the life I had to talk about?" Harte misunderstood some of what he saw, but he had the eye of a born writer for rich literary materials, and he was right in his conclusion that the South with its long and eventful history was richer than frontier California. He was both touched and amused by the Negroes whom he saw. One of the mysteries which puzzled him was the Georgia whites' "unrestrained and continual familiarity with the negro [which] has wrought between them a strange, weird sympathy and even affection which neither slavery *nor freedom* has changed, and which makes their fate almost identical."

Before the Civil War the Negro played only a small part in the literature of the South. So sensitive were the Southern people that anything one might write about the institution of slavery was liable to be misinterpreted by Abolitionists systematically combing Southern newspapers for antislavery propaganda. Few Americans realized how rich an asset the Negro was to become to American literature. Until after the Civil War few persons bothered to note down the Negro's folk tales or his songs and ballads, sinful or religious. In one sense the outcome of the War between the States may be said to have emancipated not only the slaves but the Southern writers as well. Now that slavery was a thing of the past, one could write much more freely about "the peculiar institution."

Irwin Russell of Mississippi was the first Southern writer of importance to write a vivid description of the old plantation Negro. His "Christmas-Night in the Quarters," a minor classic modeled upon Burns's "The Jolly Beggars," had an important influence upon two young writers in Virginia and Georgia, Thomas Nelson Page and Joel Chandler Harris. One can imagine the delight with which Harris early in 1878 read in that cantata Booker's ballad, a folk tale which explains that the opossum has no hairs on his tail because when Ham invented the banjo and needed strings for it,

> Dat nigger shaved 'em off as short as wash-day dinner graces;
> An' sorted ob 'em by de size, f'om little E's to basses.

Harris had discovered only a month or two earlier that the Negro folk tales were of any importance. This was when he read in *Lippincott's Magazine* for December, 1877, William Owens's "Folk-lore of the Southern Negroes." As one looks back to the time of Simms and Poe, most of our earlier Southern writers would seem to have been singularly blind to the rich literary resources of the life all around them. Often it has been a visitor from the outside—like William Cullen Bryant, William Makepeace Thackeray, Harriet Beecher Stowe, or Bret Harte—who first called attention to the literary possibilities of life in the Southern states. The first collection of Negro spirituals was compiled by three carpetbaggers, Yankee school teachers in South Carolina; and one of the first to discuss them intelligently was Colonel Thomas Wentworth Higginson, who had commanded a Negro regiment in the Union army. In September, 1866, a writer in *Scott's Monthly* of Atlanta wrote wistfully about the animal stories which as a child he had heard told by an old Negro mammy "with such gusto and Gullah grace, such animation and enthusiasm, such pantomimic illustration and imitative power!" But, he thought, no printed version of these tales would interest the reader: "Tone, emphasis, gesture, dialect, dramatic action would all be lost." If this anonymous journalist was living in 1880 when Harris brought out the first of the Uncle Remus volumes, he must have felt chagrined that he had not published these folk tales himself.

In the years that followed the Civil War the majority of our best-known writers were not college-bred, and few of them belonged to the first families of any state. Some of the best of them served an apprenticeship in a printer's shop or a newspaper office or in both, and some of them wandered far and wide as reporters or journeyman printers. Notable examples are Joel Chandler Harris, Mark Twain, Bret Harte, and William Dean Howells. On the other hand, the great majority of the early nineteenth-century authors whose names are familiar to all of us were college-bred and came from the upper circles of society. Emerson, Hawthorne, Longfellow, Holmes, Lowell, Motley, Prescott, and Parkman were gentlemen in a sense which does not apply to Walt Whitman or Joel Chandler Harris. As we look back on the New England Brahmins, the shortcomings which we associate with the genteel tradition are very apparent in much that they wrote. In a little essay entitled "Emerson's Books (The Shadows of Them)" Whitman complained of what seemed to him Emerson's "singularly dandified theory of manners." "No, no, dear friend," he exclaimed; "though the States want scholars, undoubtedly, and perhaps want ladies and gentlemen who use the bath frequently, and never laugh loud, or talk wrong, they don't want scholars, or ladies and gentlemen, at the expense of all the rest." It may well be that the fact that Whitman was not in any technical sense a gentleman enabled him to understand and interpret for us some kinds of people that Longfellow and Emerson never saw. Perhaps also the circumstances attending Harris's birth and boyhood helped to give him a deeper insight into the minds of the poorer whites and the Negro field hands than Thomas Nelson Page or James Lane Allen ever acquired.

Let me say, however, that though there are marked limitations in the outlook of our gentlemen authors of the genteel tradition, I see no necessary limitation of that kind in a writer who is also a gentleman. And here I take issue sharply with some modern critics. Among distinguished English and American authors who were gentlemen what limitation of this kind does one find in

Chaucer, Shakespeare, Fielding, Scott, Thackeray, Cooper, Hawthorne, or Simms? For that matter I do not find any great limitation in the attitude of Emerson. After all, it was he who in a famous letter greeted Whitman "at the beginning of a great career."

I wish that more of our twentieth-century writers were gentlemen of the kind that Simms was. In New York as a young man he forced a man to make a written retraction of a falsehood he had circulated about Simms's first novel. When some one suggested to Simms that he should publish the retraction in order to promote the sale of his book, he made the curt reply that he was a gentleman before he was an author. Ellen Glasgow, whose status as a Virginia lady never, I think, blinded her to the unpleasant facts of life, was in 1932 concerned lest the *Nation* send *The Sheltered Life* to "some young communist [reviewer] who judges every book by whether the author is 'well bred' or not; and regards every 'ill bred' author as 'superior.' " She added: "I was radical myself once and I am still in spots, but the bad manners Communism breeds have about cured me."

When Harris insisted that he was not a man of letters but only a "cornfield journalist," he was thinking no doubt of the apprenticeship which he had served on the *Countryman* under Joseph Addison Turner. The planter-editor's name seems significant. "Our aim," he wrote in the *Countryman,* "is to model our journal after Addison's Little Paper, The Spectator, Steele's Little Paper, The Tatler, Johnson's Little Papers, The Rambler and The Adventurer [Idler], and Goldsmith's Little Paper, The Bee. . . ." When Turner discovered that his young apprentice had literary ambitions, he gave him some excellent advice and published some of the youth's compositions in the *Countryman.* An Eatonton woman has said that once Turner laid one hand upon her head and the other on Harris's and said to them: "You will do the writing for the South that I shall be unable to do."

It was on Turner's Turnwold Plantation that Harris came by his unsurpassed knowledge of the Negroes and the rural whites. Thomas Nelson Page, who was certainly an expert witness, has said that: "No man who has ever written has known one-tenth part about the negro that Mr. Harris knows. . . ." Page's own Negro characters, fine as some of them are, are primarily accessories of the white man. I doubt whether Page knew just what his best Negro characters thought or said when no white person was near. Harris is of course past master in his handling of the dialect of the Georgia Negro. In answer to a leading question he once told Walter Hines Page that he could translate Emerson's *Essays* into Negro dialect—and Emerson was not among his favorite authors. As an example of Harris's handling of dialogue, I quote from the final chapter of *On the Plantation,* a novelette appropriately dedicated to the memory of Joseph Addison Turner. Sherman's army has just passed through Middle Georgia on its destructive march to Savannah.

In a corner of the fence, not far from the road, Joe found an old Negro woman shivering and moaning. Near her lay an old Negro man, his shoulders covered with an old ragged shawl.

> "Who is that lying there?" asked Joe.
> "It my ole man, suh."
> "What is the matter with him?"
> "He dead, suh! But, bless God, he died free!"

I can think of nothing quite like that in the writings of Harris's Southern contemporaries. Too many of them shared the old slaveholder's defensive attitude that the Negroes cared little or nothing about freedom.

Harris, who professed to regard the success of the Uncle Remus tales as "a lucky accident," once wrote to Mark Twain: " . . . I understand that my relations toward Uncle Remus are similar to those that exist between an almanac-maker and the calendar. . . ." In his reply Mark Twain assured him that the tales are literature, as of course they are even though many of them were written to fill a column on the *Atlanta Constitution* left vacant by the departure of a member of its staff. Harris had for many years dreamed of writing a novel, but he was too shy to send anything he had written to a Northern magazine or publishing house. Fortunately on the staff of the Appleton firm in New York there was J. C. Derby, who as a publisher had known and admired many Southern writers. It was he who came to Atlanta and helped Harris to make a book out of his Negro songs, sketches, and tales.

The writers of the New South were fortunate to live at a time when relations between North and South were steadily improving and when Northern readers were especially fond of Southern stories. The Southern writers were for the most part poorly educated and with few or no literary friends or advisers to help them. They began by writing, generally without pay, for Southern magazines and newspapers which struggled along for a few months or years and then expired. By and by the young Southern writers discovered that there was a lucrative literary market in the Northern cities. Richard Malcolm Johnston had given away many of his finest Georgia stories before Henry Mills Alden, editor of *Harper's Magazine,* told him that he would have published these stories and paid for them.

The Northern editors and publishers gave the Southern writers the expert advice they needed in order to put their fine materials into acceptable form. Every student remembers that Thomas Wolfe and other Scribner authors were greatly indebted to the late Maxwell Perkins, but we have forgotten that similar services were performed by Alden of *Harper's,* Thomas Bailey Aldrich of the *Atlantic Monthly,* and by Richard Watson Gilder and others on the staff of the *Century Magazine.* Without their assistance Page, Harris, James Lane Allen, George W. Cable, Grace King, Charles Egbert Craddock, and other Southern writers might never have been able to publish their stories. The grateful Harris once wrote to Robert Underwood Johnson of the *Century*: "If your kind letters fail to get good work out of a fellow, it isn't in him."

In 1885, when Harris was thirty-seven, the *Century* offered him a contract that would have permitted him to give up newspaper work. He had so little confidence in his talents that he declined the offer. He should have taken it. Fifteen years later, when he was past fifty, he did leave the *Constitution* to accept an offer from the McClure Phillips Company. By that time, however, he was too old to learn how to write a well-constructed novel.

Harris is a writer of fine tales and episodes. Few persons nowadays read any of his books except perhaps *Nights with Uncle Remus* and an occasional short story like "Free Joe." Indeed, few Southern youngsters can read Uncle Remus's dialect with any facility or much pleasure; and parents have to translate much of the dialect into American colloquial English before their children can understand and enjoy the tales. And there are too many city-bred children who do not know enough about domestic animals and life in the country to understand some of the stories. In a little book designed for small children Walt Disney or one of his illustrators pictured Brer Fox as trying to find goobers, of all places, growing on bushes and not in the ground.

The Uncle Remus tales are like *Gulliver's Travels* and some other classics in that they have a richer meaning for adults than they have for children. Uncle Remus is, like many of the old-time Negroes, a rural philosopher. For example, on one occasion he remarked: "I notices dat dem folks w'at makes a great 'miration 'bout w'at dey knows is des de folks w'ich you can't put no 'pennunce in w'en de 'casion come up." On another occasion the little boy tells about how much money one of his mother's brothers is going to make away out in Mississippi. Uncle Remus makes this comment: "Eve'y time I year folks talk 'bout makin' mo' money off dar dan dey kin anywhars nigher home, it put me in mine er de time w'en Brer Fox went huntin' de place whar dey make money." Brer Rabbit is a philosopher, too, but his view of life is not to be confused with that of Uncle Remus. When he sees that Little Mr. Cricket is about to beat Brer Fox in a race—the cricket is riding on the fox's tail—Brer Rabbit says to himself: "I'm mighty glad I met my ole fr'en kaze now I know dat all de fools ain't dead—en long may dey live fer to gimme sumpin ter do. I dunno how in de wide worril I'd git 'long widout um. Dey keeps me fat en sassy whedder craps is good er not." What living American writer of either race can capture the flavor and accent of the country Negro's speech as Harris did?

Harris's stories of the Georgia whites are often poorly constructed and for the modern reader too frequently tainted with the sentimentality which affected nearly all magazine fiction of the time; but his descriptions of rural Georgians are vivid and accurate. Better than any of his contemporaries except perhaps Mark Twain he could reproduce the speech of the rural whites. The Georgia dialect which his white characters speak is only a slightly archaic variety of the living "American language" of today. Mark Twain, who loathed the bombastic diction of Southern newspaper reporters, had the highest praise for two of his Southern writer friends: ". . . when a Southerner of genius writes modern English, his book goes upon crutches no longer, but upon wings . . . as witness the experience of Mr. Cable and 'Uncle Remus,' two of the very few Southern authors who do not write in the Southern style."

One of Harris's best characters is Billy Sanders, the overseer of Shady Dale plantation. In Page's stories the overseer is likely to turn out to be the villain, as in *Red Rock.* I do not like to think of what Erskine Caldwell or William Faulkner would have made of this shrewd and kindly Georgia cracker who, though he "would have been placed in the illiterate class by the census-taker . . . had more real knowledge and native sagacity than one-half of the people we meet every day." Billy Sanders possessed "those elemental qualities which are the basis and not the result of book education"; and he was, like Uncle Remus, a philosopher. He is no Jeeter Lester of *Tobacco Road,* nor is he one of Faulkner's numerous and contemptible Snopeses.

The story in which Billy Sanders first appears is "The Kidnapping of President Lincoln" in *On the Wing of Occasions* (1900), which deals with the Confederate secret service. Billy Sanders and his friend Francis Bethune hope to end the war in 1863 by kidnaping Lincoln and bringing him to Richmond. Billy, we soon learn, is in the story primarily to demonstrate the close resemblance between Abraham Lincoln—born in Kentucky of Virginian parents—and the true Georgia cracker. After he comes to know the President, Billy remarks: "Down our way they say you're a Yankee, but if that's so, the woods is full of Yankees in Georgia, all born an' raised right there." Harris would certainly have agreed with Walt Whitman, who in the "Death of Abraham Lincoln" had said: "Have you never realized it, my friends, that Lincoln, though grafted on the West, is essentially, in personnel and character, a Southern contribution?" In Washington Bethune and Sanders find that it would not be difficult to kidnap the President, but—and here is the sentimental flaw in the story—they like and admire Lincoln so much that, as Bethune puts it: "I would as soon kidnap my grandfather, or some one else equally dear to me."

Some years after writing "The Kidnapping of President Lincoln," Harris, at the suggestion of Walter Hines Page, revived Billy Sanders and made the "Philosopher of Shady Dale" a mouthpiece for the opinions of Editor Harris in the *Uncle Remus Magazine.* The new Billy Sanders talks sensibly enough on a great variety of topics, but he is only a pale reflection of the Sanders we first knew. In the original story Billy's talk is a delight to the listener's ear. In Washington when Stanton, the suspicious Secretary of War, asks Billy who it was that invited him to come to Washington, Billy replies:

Well, I'm like the stranger at the infair. The folks saw him hangin' roun' the door, an' some on 'em axed him what he was doin' there, an' he said, says he, "I heard the fiddlin' an' the shufflin', an' smelt the dram, an' I jest thought I'd look on an' see well done done well."

The subject of my lectures is Southern Life in Fiction, but I cannot speak of the literature of the New South without saying something about Sidney Lanier, who was a native of this city and as fine an example of the gentleman of the nineteenth-century South as one can find in Virginia or Georgia. Lanier's writings and his reputation were also very dear to Mrs. Lamar, who endowed this series of lectures. Lanier published only one novel; and though it contains some fine passages, he soon came to regard *Tiger-Lilies* as a failure. And yet some of his early dialect poems and his superb ballad, "The Revenge of Hamish," reveal a narrative gift; and if he had chosen, he might in the course of time have written successful novels and short stories about the Georgia people whom he knew and loved so well. Like Harris and Mark Twain, he had a fine ear for the niceties of Southern speech. In "Uncle Jim's Baptist Revival-Hymn"—though his brother Clifford may have had a hand in this poem—the Negro dialect is recorded with a skill that few of Lanier's contemporaries could have equaled.

> De jaybird squeal to de mockin'-bird: "Stop!
> Don' gimme none o' yo' sass;
> Better sing one song for de Baptis' crop,
> *Dey's mightily in de grass, grass,*
> *Dey's mightily in de grass."*

At the time when Lanier determined to devote his energies to poetry, the old New England poets had all written their best work; Whitman was unpopular; and Emily Dickinson, unknown. The lesser poets were turning out conventional verses of which the chief use was to fill up the otherwise blank half-pages in the magazines. When Lanier was released from the Federal prison at Point Lookout in Maryland in 1865, he had the germs of tuberculosis in his lungs and only sixteen years to live—and that at a time when, as he wrote to Bayard Taylor ten years afterwards: "Perhaps you know that with us of the younger generation in the South since the War, pretty much the whole of life has been merely not-dying!" The life of a poet anywhere in the world is likely to be a lonely one, and except for his father and his brother Lanier had almost no one with whom he could discuss his poems, no one to give him the kind of craftsman's criticism which he finally got first from Paul Hamilton Hayne and later from Bayard Taylor. One can only admire the courage that Lanier displayed when he continued to write poetry in spite of poverty and all kinds of discouragement. It was a courageous philosophy that he expressed in a poem entitled "Opposition":

> Of fret, of dark, of thorn, of chill,
> Complain no more; for these, O heart,
> Direct the random of the will
> As rhymes direct the rage of art.

Lanier died over three-quarters of a century ago, but the critics are still far from agreement as to his rank among our American poets. Many of his poems are unfinished. He was an improviser who, unlike Poe, rarely polished any poem to perfection. A strain of sentimentality seems to some critics to vitiate much of his work. In recent years some students have been either indifferent or hostile to those poets who, like Spenser, Milton, Coleridge, Shelley, Keats, Tennyson, and Yeats, have striven for verbal melody. They forget that word music is one of the characteristics which distinguish poetry from prose, and it is also a chief means by which the poet, like a magician, casts his spell upon the reader. In a short story entitled "Wireless" Rudyard Kipling said in effect that in all English poetry " . . . there are no more than five–five little lines–of which one can say: 'These are the pure Magic. These are the clear Vision. The rest is only poetry.' " There are of course more than five such lines to be found in each of the poets whom I have just named, and there are a few such memorable lines in the best poems of Lanier. He attached great importance to the message which as a poet he might give to the world, but I am more impressed by his verbal melody and by his power to make us see the beauty of the Georgia landscape. One finds musical lines in all of his best poems. Among those that are less familiar I particularly like this stanza from "The Cloud":

> Sail on, sail on, fair cousin Cloud;
> Oh, loiter hither from the sea.
>   Still-eyed and shadow-brow'd,
> Steal off from yon far-drifting crowd,
> And come and brood upon the marsh with me.

Better known is the "Song of the Chattahoochee," in which the poet handles place names with something of the skill with which Milton employed them in *Paradise Lost.*

>   High o'er the hills of Habersham,
>   Veiling the valleys of Hall,
> The hickory told me manifold
> Fair tales of shade, the poplar tall
> Wrought me her shadowy self to hold,
> The chestnut, the oak, the walnut, the pine,
> Overleaning, with flickering meaning and sign,
> Said, *Pass not, so cold, these manifold*
>   *Deep shades of the hills of Habersham,*
>   *These glades in the valleys of Hall.*

Unlike that earlier Georgia poet, Thomas Holley Chivers, Lanier does not sacrifice sense to sound. In "A Ballad of Trees and the Master" there is one graphic line which makes us see the olive trees.

> Into the woods my Master went
>   Clean forspent, forspent.
> Into the woods my Master came,
>   Forspent with love and shame.
> But the olives they were not blind to Him,
> The little gray leaves were kind to Him:
> The thorn-tree had a mind to Him
>   When into the woods He came.

Much of the best in Lanier's later poetry deals with the Marshes of Glynn. There are in the Southern states many marshes and swamps, and they figure in stories and poems by Simms, Mrs. Stowe, Cable, Kate Chopin, and other writers; but of them all no one has captured the beauty of the marsh country in a way to rival Lanier. The marsh country is like the Western plains in that a visitor must linger there awhile before he can enjoy its beauty and feel its grandeur. English writers of the caliber of Dickens, Stevenson, and Kipling were all repelled by the vastness and the nakedness of the Western prairies. It remained for American writers—Bryant, Mark Twain, Willa Cather, and others—to reveal to us the beauty of what seemed to the Britishers only endless and empty spaces. If I had never read Lanier's Marsh poems, I fear that I should have driven through the coastal country around Brunswick with only a casual glance at the Marshes of Glynn. As it is, for me as for many another visitor Lanier has vividly pictured a region which I shall hope to see again and again. He has added yet another memorable locality to Tarrytown, Boston Common, the bridge at Concord, and the battle-fields around Richmond on which he courageously played his part as a Confederate soldier. No one who has read Lanier and seen the Georgia coast can ever quite forget the magical lines in which he has described "the length and the breadth of the marvellous marshes of Glynn."

In these lectures I have not said much about the rich and varied Southern fiction of the twentieth century; and if I have seemed to some of my listeners too exclusively concerned with our earlier literature, it is in part because these lectures, by Mrs. Lamar's wishes, were designed to help us to preserve the best in our Southern cultural traditions. These traditions were developed in the eighteenth and nineteenth centuries, which today seem increasingly remote from our contemporary interests.

For Willa Cather, who, though one thinks of her as a Nebraskan, was born in Virginia, "The world broke in two in 1922 or thereabouts"; and, as she said in *Not under Forty* (1936), the people she was writing about in that book "slid back into yesterday's seven thousand years." The South is changing so rapidly and we are losing our sense of the past so steadily that we are in danger of forgetting our origins and the ideals and the achievements of our predecessors. The ideals which we have inherited did not simply happen; they came as the result of high aims and hard work on the part of many men and women. We need, for example, to remember more often than we do the large part which Southern soldiers and statesmen had in making Americans a free people and in establishing the form of government under which it has operated for the better part of two centuries. I wish especially that our political leaders had a larger endowment of that keen sense of history which has actuated Sir Winston Churchill throughout his career and made of him not only a great statesman embodying the finest of England's traditional ideals but also a historian worthy of the tradition established by Macaulay, John Richard Green, and the Trevelyans.

In our time new and momentous scientific discoveries have come in such numbers and followed so quickly on the heels of one another that it is difficult for even the well-educated man to feel that he can afford to take the time to inform himself about the historical development of the region in which he lives. Yet the test of the educated man is his ability to look before and after and imaginatively to live in the past and the future as well as in the present. There is a provincialism of time as well as of place, and it is the former that we in an academic community—and at Mercer you have one of the finest—must do our utmost to combat. If we are to preserve our sense of continuity with the Southern past, then it is the educated men and women of this section who must see to it that the best in that past is kept alive. This we must do without ignoring its shortcomings or idealizing that past out of all resemblance to the actuality. It is good for us to remember that in Virginia, in Georgia, and in other Southern states there once lived such men as Thomas Jefferson, Robert E. Lee, and Sidney Lanier. We shall be better Americans if we remember them. There are many Georgians whose memories I hope you will continue to cherish—among them, the trio described by Joel Chandler Harris as "Robert Toombs, impetuous and imperious; Ben Hill, impressive and genial; Alexander Stephens, pallid and frail, but with the fires of vitality burning in his eyes."

We must not, however, permit ourselves to become reactionaries or professional Southerners. The Southern states are now an integral part of a great nation, which owes an immense debt to such Southerners as James Madison and Woodrow Wilson. Since Lee surrendered his little army at Appomattox in April, 1865, the South has seen its sons march off to fight in four wars: in Cuba and the Philippines, twice in Germany and France, in the South Pacific, and in Korea. We are now Americans first and Georgians and Virginians afterwards.

One thing more. I might in these lectures have chosen to say more about those elements in our Southern traditions which we would be happier without. I do not wish any of you to feel that I find no shortcomings in either the Old or the Newer South. There are many of them. But it is better to fix our attention on what is worthy of imitation; and these lectures by the terms of Mrs. Lamar's bequest are rightly dedicated to "the permanent preservation of the values of Southern culture, history, and literature." It is a worthy aim, and I am glad to have been able to contribute something toward the achievement of that end.

Selected Bibliography

Herbert R. Brown, "The Great American Novel," *American Literature,* VII (March, 1935), 1-14.

William Alfred Bryan, *George Washington in American Literature, 1775-1865*. New York: Columbia University Press, 1952.

Alexander Cowie, *The Rise of the American Novel.* New York: American Book Company, 1948.

Donald Davidson, *The Attack on Leviathan.* Chapel Hill: University of North Carolina Press, 1938.

Southern Writers in the Modern World. Athens: University of Georgia Press, 1958.

Still Rebels, Still Yankees and Other Essays. Baton Rouge: Louisiana State University Press, 1957.

Bernard DeVoto, "Interrelations of History and Literature," *Approaches to American Social History*. New York: D. Appleton-Century Company, 1937. Edited by William Ezra Lingelbach.

A. T. Dickinson, Jr., *American Historical Fiction.* New York: Scarecrow Press, 1958.

Douglas Southall Freeman. *The South to Posterity: An Introduction to the Writing of Confederate History.* New York: Charles Scribner's Sons, 1939.

Francis Pendleton Gaines, *The Southern Plantation: A Study in the Development and the Accuracy of a Tradition.* New York: Columbia University Press, 1924.

Ellen Glasgow, *A Certain Measure: An Interpretation of Prose Fiction*. New York: Harcourt, Brace & Company, 1943.

Will N. Harben, "American Backgrounds for Fiction: Georgia," *The Bookman*, XXXVIII (October, 1913), 186-192.

Ima Honaker Herron, *The Small Town in American Literature*. Durham: Duke University Press, 1939.

Jay Broadus Hubbell, *The South in American Literature, 1607-1900*. Durham: Duke University Press, 1954.

"Cavalier and Indentured Servant in Virginia Fiction," *South Atlantic Quarterly*, XXVI (January, 1927), 22-39.

"The Smith-Pocahontas Story in Literature," *Virginia Magazine of History and Biography*, LXV (July, 1957), 275-300.

C. P. Lee, "Decline and Death of the Southern Gentleman," *Southwest Review*, XXXVI (Summer, 1951), 164-170.

Ernest Erwin Leisy, *The American Historical Novel*. Norman: University of Oklahoma Press, 1950.

Robert A. Lively, *Fiction Fights the Civil War*. Chapel Hill: University of North Carolina Press, 1957.

Bernard Mayo, *Myths and Men: Patrick Henry, George Washington, Thomas Jefferson*. Athens: University of Georgia Press, 1959.

John Herbert Nelson, *The Negro Character in American Literature*. Lawrence: University of Kansas, 1926.

Frank Lawrence Owsley, *Plain Folk of the Old South*. Baton Rouge: Louisiana State University Press, 1949.

Thomas James Pressly, *Americans Interpret Their Civil War*. Princeton: Princeton University Press, 1954.

Arthur Hobson Quinn, *American Fiction: An Historical and Critical Survey*. New York: D. Appleton-Century Company, 1936.

Elmer E. Stoll, "Literature No 'Document,'" *Modern Language Review*, XIX (April, 1924), 141-157.

Willard Thorp, *A Southern Reader*. New York: Alfred A. Knopf, 1955.

John Donald Wade, *Augustus Baldwin Longstreet: A Study of the Development of Culture in the South*. New York: The Macmillan Company, 1924.

Dixon Wecter, *The Hero in America: A Chronicle of Hero-Worship*. New York: Charles Scribner's Sons, 1941.

Louis Booker Wright, *The First Gentlemen of Virginia: Intellectual Qualities of the Early Colonial Ruling Class*. San Marino, California: Huntington Library, 1940.

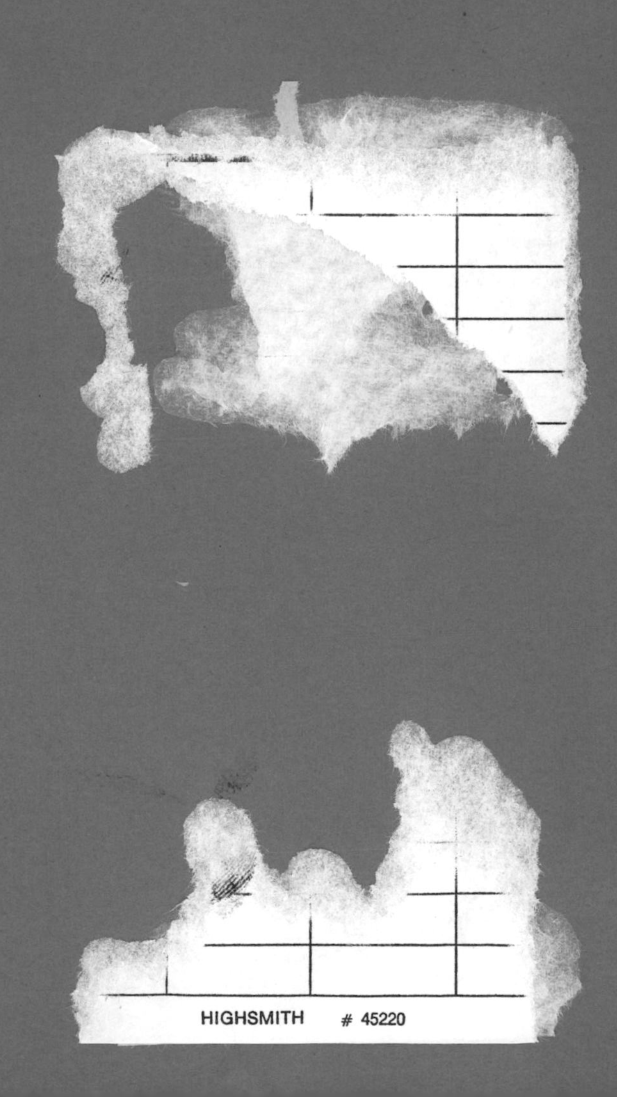
HIGHSMITH # 45220